Would You Like To Be Jewish?

Dr. Akiva Gamliel Belk

- FOUNDER OF -

jewishpath.org • 7commands.com • bnti.us

B'nai Noach Torah Institute, LLC

Contact us at:

talk@bnti.us

Copyright © 2013

Dr. Akiva Gamliel Belk

All rights reserved

ISBN-13: 978-0615762647

ISBN -10: 0615762646

Publisher
B'nai Noach Torah Institute, LLC
Post Office Box 14
Cedar Hill, Missouri 63016
talk@bnti.us
First Edition 02-03-2013

DEDICATION

A Light Rekindled
By Dr. Akiva Gamliel Belk

Oft in generations past a fervent alluring magnificent light glowed,

This burst of light revealed many dedicated hours of Torah lines rowed,

Word by Word each line carefully considered as Torah illumination flowed,

Oh, the pleasure of learning the Holy Text on the table by the fire showed.

Blessed are the generations where dedicated love of Torah is bestowed,

*Then something awful happened. Our love
and dedication for Torah slowed*

*From one generation to the next the
glorious Torah was allowed to Erode*

*Now, with teared eyes, generations later I
search for the path relatives strode*

*The once great light of Torah is only a spark
when blowed*

*Then something really wonderful happens
the spark of Torah light again glowed.*

*A rise oh Hope of blessed light. Set us
aright in the path our relatives strode.*

FORWARD

Making out my grocery list is always daunting. Trying to remember everything that should get written down. I get in the car, drive to the store. I park the car, enter the store and look for my list. Wouldn't you know it, I forgot the list. So many things to remember. Such a short time between when I have written the list and when at the store trying to remember what was on the list. I go up and down each isle trying to see if something that I see will spark my memory. Returning home I look at my list and see I have forgotten several things on it.

When we read books that are inspired we have a great expectation that they were written by people who have a much better memory than myself. I was on a search my whole life for a way to be close to God. My paths in this search were varied and sometimes very challenging. My ancestry is Jewish but I was not Observant. I tried various religious paths in this search.

Searching for God, searching for Truth was very difficult. I accepted some teachings and then after years of study found that there were errors. There were many learned, intelligent people who had studied and written on what they thought was Truth. I bought book after book trying to find someone who could answer my questions. Eventually I found the Truth I sought. Judaism is not a religion. It is a way of living, a way of living as God has asked us to do.

Dr. Akiva Gamliel in a very simple yet deep way shows us the path to truth. I have to be honest, Dr. Akiva Gamliel is my husband. He writes at all hours of the day and night. I will wake up sometime during the night to find him gone and after listening a bit, I hear the click-clack-click of his keyboard in the office. He has many degrees and has studied many years with some great teachers. He has a passion for truth. His passion to help people never seems to diminish.

In my journey - searching for Truth - I found that there are some people who are not open to questions. Some who are educated but still closed to what the Truth is. What you get from their teachings, their books is their version of the Truth. How can there be different versions of Truth? I was just not satisfied with this mindset. I kept searching and searching. I had been alone for almost 20 years when I found Dr. Akiva Gamliel at BNTI.US. He was to say the least very challenging. What impressed me so much was that he had references for everything he said. I could look up and study these references for myself. Mulling them over in my mind, researching more - perusing the internet for information. I found that what he wrote about the Christian Writings was True. I had been leaning towards that fact for several years but could not put all the pieces of the puzzle together in my mind. It was very difficult doing an about face in my concepts of God, Salvation and the after life.

This book **Do You Want To Be Jewish** is for those people who may not understand what it means to be Jewish. It is also for those who do want to be Jewish. This book focuses on Truth.

Your beliefs will be challenged, your concepts of who God really is and what He expects from you will also be challenged. Challenged but in a gentle non aggressive way. No one should be afraid of Truth. After all God **IS** Truth. Those who really want to know God will never be afraid of seeking the Truth.

My journey continues. Come and join me now, read this book and see if you heart truly seeks God. There is only ONE God. Seek Him with all your heart and you will find Him.

This book is your next step on your quest to know, love and serve God Almighty.

Brachah Rivkah 'Revi' Belk

Would You Like To Be JEWISH?

Table of Contents

DEDICATION..5
PREFACE..13
ACKNOWLEDGEMENTS................................17
INTRODUCTION..19
Chapter One..37
   Observances / Obligations.........................37
Chapter Two..41
   Observances..41
Chapter Three..49
   Good Self Governing..................................49
Chapter Four..59
   PERCEPTION..59
Chapter Five..79
   Disinformation..79
Chapter Six...113

613 Observances	113
Chapter Seven	121
Vision / Inspiration	121
Chapter Eight	131
Sefer Torah	131
Chapter Nine	139
Comparing Writers	139
Chapter Ten	147
Truth	147
ABOUT THE AUTHOR	155

PREFACE

Dear Reader this is the first Book of a series that I intend to do if our Creator is Willing. My intent was to take subjects of discomfort between Judaism and other religions and to talk these over with the readers. Sometimes, it helps to put sensitive issues in writing. It also help to give some background. When one writes they have what they have written to refresh their memory. One should provide references. I am VERY BIG about insisting on references. Requiring references is good sound tradition among Rabbis. When one writes on a subject they need to backup what they have written with references.

I don't want to be perceived as hard, unforgiving or as bossy. Yet, I am going to quote references in this book from many different sources. When I quote a reference DON'T BLOW IT OFF! Every reference should be carefully checked.

Dear reader if you want to be Jewish or

understand Judaism these references will open up worlds of powerful powerful study. When a reader checks out the references it says to me that the reader is serious. It says the reader wants to know Truth. There are so many that just believe. It is rare if they question anything. Once I was among this group.

The subjects we explore are INTENDED to CHALLENGE! My youngest son taught me something about challenging ones self. Joel was a very disciplined runner. He had a routine he kept religiously! I only remember parts. He got up early. He stretched. He ran for miles. He drank water. He stayed away from soda pop. He didn't smoke. He required noodle dishes often. He worked out hard. When Joel was in pain from his rigorous training he smiled! He has a beautiful smile! He laughed and he sucked it up. Joel trained for a fourth of July race in our town. This was a very big event. There were runners everywhere. I was so proud of Joel. It was easy to see which runners were well trained. As Joel was doing his stretches I walked up to ask him who he though his competition would be? He stopped stretching for a few seconds and pointed out about seven runners. He said something like each of these fellows are gong to be really tuff. He said, his only chance was to press them as hard as he could. I wished Joel luck. I prayed for his success. Everyone lined up. The race began. Joel was out in front like a flash. After some distance he pulled away from everyone. This was a long race at high altitude for a kid from sunny beaches and sea level. The runners were out of sight for a very long time. Then they turned the corner. There was Joel still leading everyone. It was about four blocks to the finish line. Only several runners had any chance of catching him. I was so proud!! As it turn out two runners in the final 100 feet caught him. It was back and forth for a little while but they had more stamina than Joel and eventually pulled ahead. They did not blow by him. Joel took a third place. When the race finished. A short while later these well trained runners were all around Joel. They were hugging him and telling him they though they were going to loose the race. They tried to catch him earlier but could not catch him. It was then they realized he was for real. They wanted to know who he was. They wanted to know all about him.

Dear Reader I study with dedication. There are times I have lost track of days and nights... Why? I want to know the Truth. Knowing the Truth comes at a cost. Are you dedicated? I have written this book hoping to attract those who *'just believe'* out of retirement... out of their sleep... out of their lull. This is an easy book to read and understand but it will challenge you! Don't set this book down with out checking the references. I am not frightened by questions... In the Yeshiva world a Rabbi expects to be challenged often. My God Bless my Rabbis!!

ACKNOWLEDGEMENTS

Thank God for the many Blessing bestowed upon me, upon Revi and upon our children, our grandchildren and great grand children. We are thankful for His blessings!

The greatest blessing a man can have is a good wife and Aizer, a Helpmate. Dear Reader, my wife helps to make everything I do possible. Kaw Naw Nah Haw Raw. She is the leader of our home. Brachah means blessing and Rivkah means 'Greatly Honored'. The first two letters, [רב] the ר Reish and the ב Bet mean 'Great' and 'Honored'. The last two Letters mean [קה] mean to be blunt to get to the point quickly.

When Revi and I wed she was quiet and to the point. Revi gets to the point when something needs to be done. Revi says this is a trait passed on from from her father, may he rest in peace. He father was known for being a man of few words. Revi says about the longest conversation she had with her father was maybe two minutes.

Our Creator also chooses a few Words to communicate. When we choose the correct words it only takes a few words.

Thank you Revi...

Dr. Akiva Gamliel

INTRODUCTION

After nineteen years of marriage Passover would be very different this year. Our Family was experiencing division and separation. I lived in a small studio apartment where the neighbor next door and I shared the only bathroom. The rent was around $182.00 per month including electric, gas, water, sewer etc. The boys and their mother lived in the family home in the suburbs of Denver. The boys would visit every other weekend.

It was especially difficult this year because we would not have our own Passover Sedar. Joshua our older son would be with his mother doing his thing. Joel our younger son would be with me sharing Passover as a guest of our Rabbi and his lovely family. Before Passover it is necessary to clean one's house, apartment, office, auto etc. as best as one can. That year I owned so little. Passover cleaning took an afternoon. The kitchen area was about 6' wide by 8'. long. The bedroom area was 1 chest of drawers, a single bed and a make shift closet. There was a two burner stove. The oven was tiny. The Refrigerator was maybe 9 cubic feet with a freezer the size of two large yellow page books. At the opposite end was a kitchen table, several chairs, a gas heater and a lamp next to a single front room chair.

Joel's cleaning assignment was the bedroom. My cleaning area was the kitchen. Any money in pants pockets or coats, under the bed in and around the dresser was Joel's if he found some. Joel found some change and maybe several dollars. To this day Joel claims I told him I lost a twenty dollar bill. I don't recall that. Perhaps Joel was making reference to an incident years earlier when as a sailor I lost $20.00. Maybe we talked about this sailor story while driving from the family home... How these type of things get twisted around only God Knows.

After a really good job of Passover cleaning Joel expressed disappointment that he didn't find the $20.00. I asked, 'What Twenty Dollars?'

Joel replied, 'You know Dad, the Twenty dollars you lost.'

Son, I didn't loose twenty dollars... Yes you did... Dear Readers, I felt bad. My son was disappointed. It appeared to be my fault. Unfortunately I did not have even twenty dollars to help smooth this out... It was a misunderstanding. Misunderstandings happen. Misunderstandings can be the source for many hurts and disappointments. False perceptions and mistaken ideas can be the initiator for choosing the wrong path time after time. Misunderstanding directions causes many of us to drive miles out of the way every week. It's so easy! Two family members can experience a misunderstanding that can cause each family to choose a different direction. It may take years to reconcile the misunderstanding. I am saying it is easy to misread a situation. It happens all the time. When misunderstandings happen the truth can be pushed aside or buried in lies. We see this happen frequently with news broadcasts and publications.

Misunderstandings are very serious! Misunderstandings are difficult to avoid. I think the readers of this book will have an entirely different understanding of Judaism after some common misunderstandings are cleared up.

Do you know the history of the destruction of Jerusalem? The destruction of Jerusalem came about through a misunderstanding. There was a man who had a friend named Kamza and an enemy named Bar Kamza. He made a party. He instructed his servant, to invite Kamza. Instead the servant by mistake invited his enemy, Bar Kamza. When the man [who gave the party] found Bar Kamza there he said, '*What are you doing here? Get out*'.

Bar Kamza said, '*[please] since I am already here, let me stay, and I will pay you for whatever I eat and drink*'.

He said, '*I won't.*

Bar Kamza said, *'then let me give you half the*

cost of the party'.

'No', he said.

Bar Kamza said, *['please] then let me pay for the whole party'.*

He still said, *'No',* and he took him by the hand and put him out.

Bar Kamza thought that since the Rabbis were sitting there and did not stop him, this shows that they agreed with him. I will go and inform against them, to the Government. He went and said to the Emperor, *'The Jews are rebelling against you'.*

The Emperor questioned, *'How can I tell?'*

Bar Kamza said, *'Send them an offering and see whether they will offer it on the altar'.* So he sent with him a fine calf. While on the way Bar Kamza made a blemish on its upper lip, in a place where it is counted as a blemish. The Rabbis did not offer the calf because of the blemish.

As a result the Emperor sent Nero against Jerusalem then Vespasian who besieged the Holy City for three years. Eventually Jerusalem was destroyed.

The Bible has many varying interpretations. We will examine some of these expositions and seek a greater clarity so you will know if you would like to be Jewish. We will discuss concepts and share why one is likely to become Jewish and another is not.

Chapter one will summarize what Jews are supposed to believe. We will list thirteen concepts of Judaism. We will then discuss some of these concepts throughout the pages of this book. While on the one hand we are discovering what Judaism is on the other hand we are going to share what Judaism is not. We are going to review some common misunderstandings about what other religions say the Bible Teaches regarding Judaism. We will evaluate and analyze disinformation. I will communicate observances that the Torah portion of the Bible Teaches Jews / The Children of Israel to live by. Yet, this book is NOT an exhaustive study! It is a beginning for some. There are Five areas that I feel are of great importance. First, what are the principles of Judaism? What do we believe? The first chapter will define our beliefs. The reader will be able to refer back to the first chapter as we discuss important observances within Judaism. Second, are the silent areas. These are areas of the Bible religions normally do not discuss. The information in the silent areas will be very important and informative to the reader. After reviewing the silent areas the reader may feel a greater closeness to Judaism. Third, are areas of misunderstandings. Fourth ,are areas of disinformation. Fifth, how this is relevant to us.

As we approach the day when Moshiach / Messiah will come we realize that the Messiah will come much sooner than most of us think. Yet, when we look around our world there is so much religious indifference and hatred between religions, ethic groups and peoples. One has to wonder, how all this is going to get worked out. Yet, issues will get worked out quickly. World problems are very great. Yet, there are answers and resolutions that will correct every issue and usher in world peace. It could begin with you reading this book.

Why did I title this book <u>Would You Like To Be Jewish?</u> This goes to the fifth point relevance. It is for an important reason. 3,325 years ago the Nation of Israel stood before the Lord God on Mount Sinai to receive the Ten Commandments and all other related Commandments. There are a total of 613 Commands. In addition to the Children of Israel standing on Mount Sinai to receive the 613 Commands every Jewish Soul that will ever exist in this world also stood on Mount Sinai to receive the 613 Commands. In addition to these the souls of millions of non-Jews that will convert to Judaism, also stood on Mount Sinai to receive the 613 Commands. If you were there then this book should be very relevant .

This is where several serious issues lay. Judaism used to be evangelical but that changed with rabbinical decree prohibiting evangelism. Abraham converted thousands to Judaism. How do we know this? Look at Genesis 14.14. How many trained servants were born in Abraham's house? Each had a mother, father and sister. This was at least 1,272 individuals. At that time Abraham was young. He would evangelize for dozens of years. Many more would convert to Judaism.

Reader the dilemma is Jews are not supposed to evangelize yet there are untold thousands maybe millions of non-Jews that stood at Mount Sinai and took upon themselves the obligation to Observe the 613 Commands of The Torah Portion of the Bible. Everyone of these MUST CONVERT to Judaism. The Rabbis know this. Many Jews know this. Did you know this? We discuss this. Yet, I have to walk a fine line. I cannot come across as evangelical. I cannot encourage you to convert to Judaism. Is this a problem? I can tell the truth. I can discuss misunderstandings. I can set the record straight. I discuss areas of apprehension with regards to sin, salvation, repentance, Heaven and the life after. I review some inaccurate and false teachings by other religions regarding what the Torah portion of the Bible says. I draw attention to Biblical Teachings that are ignored and that are lost in translation. IT IS SURPRISING!!

Misunderstandings… Wow!

Within the writings of this book I will use the term *the Torah Portion of the Bible*. It is important to understand what I am doing. My purpose is to remind the reader that the Torah is part of the Bible. I do not want to isolate the Torah from being a part of the Bible.

We will use a number of Jewish terms followed by a forward slash defining the Word used.

Aleph to Tav - [א ת] When I use the words *from Aleph to Tav*, I mean *from the first Letter of* *the Aleph Bet, the Letter Aleph [א] to the last Letter of the Aleph Bet, the Letter Tav [ת]. The Eht represents being all inclusive from the beginning of one letter to the conclusion of another letter. The word Et is spelled Alef Tav, the first and last letters of the Hebrew alphabet. It therefore implies a transition from beginning to end. Rabbi Ishmael therefore states that its main purpose [in the instance he is referring to] is to indicate the transitive sense of the word "created."*

Rabbi Akiba, on the other hand replies that the very fact that Et contains the Alef Tav implies that it superimposes the entire alphabet between the subject verb and the predicated noun adding all things that pertain to that noun (Cf. Or Torah, Bereisheit). See <u>The Bahir</u> pp 108, 109

In Chapter Two we share some straight talk that borders on the silent areas. Chapter two also borders between misunderstanding and disinformation. This depends on what you know and what you do with what you know. In the

Torah portion of the Bible we learn of the Word מִצְוַת Mizvat, meaning obligation. Depending upon one's religious affiliation, one might refer to Mitzvat as a Command, as The Law, as the Law of Moses, as precepts and so forth. Our goal in Chapter two is to show there have always been Obligations for humankind to follow. Following Obligations are not difficult. It is not living the life of a legalist.

In Chapter Three we discuss good self governing. I state, 'There was a time when I would not want the walls of my home to speak of what they heard and saw'. Yet, with repentance one reaches the place of good self governing when the walls of ones home glisten with purity and righteousness, Kaw Nah Naw Hah Raw. Righteous Individual Responsibility / Good Self Governing is possibly the most important Observance of the Bible. Our first parents failed to employ good self governing when dealing with the serpent. Any of us can make the same mistake, Kaw Naw Nah Haw Raw! Even atheists who say they do not believe in God obey His Laws.

Chapter Four is a discussion on our perception. How do the teachings in the Christian Scriptures impact our impression of Judaism? Many Christian Messianic's claim to be Jewish and claim to believe Jesus is the Messiah. I use the word believe because the Christian Scriptures actually teach Jesus is NOT the Jewish Messiah. One does not have to stretch at all. The teachings are very clear. You will see right out of the pages of the Christian Scriptures that it is impossible for Jesus to be the Jewish Messiah. I expect this chapter to be dramatic for anyone who believes Jesus is the Messiah. This chapter will change your life forever! After you study through this chapter you will be devastated. You will be wondering what am I going to do from here?

In Chapter Five we discuss disinformation and confusion. We discuss the entomology of Religions of the world. Religions of the world

MUST STOP using painful hurtful terms in communication. Terms like Old Testament, New Testament, NOT INSPIRED BY GOD and not a part of the Inspiration of The Bible!! They reflect the prejudice of men and religions. They should not be the heading one sees first in Books written to reflect truth and righteousness. Terms like Hebrew Scriptures, Christian Writings or Christian Bible are preferred. Terms like Old and New lack truthfulness. We need to be truthful. We need to come together. There is no contest here. We love God and want to serve him. Let's do so in a way that produces positive results.

Chapter Six continues with a discussion of Catholic and Christian teachings that the Perfect Torah of the Lord is done away with? This is ridiculous! Why? The Christian Writings quote the Words, 'it is written' over 75 times, the Word, 'Scripture' over 30 times and the Word Scriptures over 20 times? At the time of their chronological writing each were making reference to the Hebrew Scripture. None of these Verses were making reference to the Christian Writings. My writings are not anti Catholic or anti Christian. I am just saying, 'People get real!' Think about what you are doing. What value is there in this? I point out fallacies. Dear Reader where are the prophecies regarding the end of days found? Where are the prophecies regarding Moshiach / Messiah found? Where is EVERY instruction regarding tithing found? Where are the battles of Armageddon found? Where is the seventy weeks discussed? The answer is in the Hebrew Scriptures.

The discussion in Chapter Seven turns to communication with God. It is not common place to hear the Voice of The Lord. Even Moses during the twelve months while struggling, for the Children Of Israel's freedom in Egypt, ONLY received limited communication from the Lord. The Lord and Moses communicated 29 times. Yet, even though Moses was on the highest level of prophecy, communication with the Lord was very limited.
In Chapter Eight we discus what it is like to be a Scribe of the Bible. The purpose of going into

these details is to make the reader aware of the Holiness and the Separation a Scribe takes upon himself. I know a Scribe. We visited often when he lived in America. He practiced these customs. He went to a special school where he was taught how to be a scribe. He met with me and shared about the duties and responsibilities of a scribe, he wanted me to become a sofer – a scribe.

Moses was greater than any of the scribes in the past or in the future.

In Chapter nine we compare a tiny amount of information of what we know about the Writers of the Hebrew Scriptures and the Writers of the Christian Testament. We do this because most individuals have not stopped to think about the Writers and the influence they carry. If one is going to make outlandish claims that one book is done and the other Book is not they had better be able to answer serious questions in this chapter. We will examine which makes more sense. Superiority of one book is clear based upon the writers.

In Chapter Ten we write about Truth. Each religion believes it has the Truth. With limited knowledge we can see that God designed a plan for the earth to follow. God designed a plan for our bodies to follow. It is therefore reasonable to expect God to have a plan from the beginning for humankind to follow. Knowing this we should be able to understand that an organized God would not Create Adam and Eve without a plan. We may debate what God's Plan is but we recognize God has a plan. Just because we may not know about God's plan does NOT mean it did not exist. If other religions do not speak of God's Plan From The Beginning that does not mean there was no plan. The Truth is, God Has always had a plan. In these first ten chapters we have shown many possibilities from different angles. Each shows that God had a plan. We have provided a number of references that establish a plan existed. We have also proven the absolute absurdity of the teachings from other religions which say the Hebrew Scriptures are fulfilled, done away with and are not longer valid for our time.

Chapter One

Observances / Obligations

Dear Reader the following thirteen Principles are concepts. Our approach to the question of would you like to be Jewish is from a conceptual base rather than a list of observances. We review the broader picture. We learn the concept before we learn the specifics. So, we are providing a list of thirteen concepts that we will draw upon in discussions throughout this book.

- Praised and Exalted Is the Living God -

1.) He Exists -- unbounded by time Is His Existence.

2.) He Is One -- and there is no unity like His Oneness. His Oneness Is Incomprehensible and Infinite.

3.) He has no semblance of a body. He does not

have physical form. There is no comparison to His Holiness.

4.) He Preceded every being that was created -- He Is the First. Nothing precedes His Precedence.

5.) He Is the Master of the Universe to every creature. He Manifests His Greatness and His Supremacy.

6.) He Gave His Prophecies to His treasured splendrous people.

7.) In Israel none like Moses arose again. He is a prophet who clearly perceived His Vision.

8.) God Gave the Torah of Truth through His Prophet, the most trusted of His household, containing the 613 Precepts of the Bible to His People. Everyone has an obligation to Observe certain precepts.

9.) God Will Never amend nor exchange His

Torah for another, for all eternity.

10.) He Carefully Examines and Knows our hidden most secrets; He Perceives a matter's outcome at its origin.

11.) He Rewards man with Kindness according to his deed; He Places evil on the wicked according to his wickedness.

12.) By the End of Days He Will Send our Messiah, to redeem those longing for His Final Salvation.

13.) God Will Revive the dead in His Abundant Kindness -- Blessed is His Praised Name forever.

SUMMARY – The Thirteen Concepts Teach belief in God, The legitimacy of *The Torah Portion* of the Bible, human responsibility and our rewards for obedience.

Chapter Two

Observances

The Eighth Concept Teaches human responsibility.

God Gave the Torah of Truth through His Prophet, the most trusted of His household, **containing the 613 Precepts of the Bible for us, His People. Everyone has an obligation to Observe certain precepts.**

What does your religion teach about the beginning of humankind? Does your religion teach that the Creator Instructed humankind in Observances he wanted them to follow? Did Adam and Eve know there were Obligations God required them to Observe? Did Adam and Eve understand the difference between right and wrong? How did humankind come to establish governments, and courts, and police forces, and laws? Does your religion teach that The Lord God Breathed into humankind the breath of life and from that point forward we became a living soul? Our living soul has emotions, feelings and a thought processes. God could have used a creation process requiring millions of years or just the blink of an eye. We are not studying the time factor here. Our concern is that there were Obligations in place for us to follow and that we could understand them. Did these obligations have anything to do with being Jewish? No! Adam was not Jewish. Eve was not Jewish. Cain and his wife were not Jewish. Able and his wives were not Jewish. Seth and his wives were not Jewish.

From the beginning of creation God Revealed to humankind 613 Observances that cover every aspect of life in this universe. The 613 Observances were given <u>EXCLUSIVELY</u> to the Children of Israel on Mount Sinai 2,449 years later yet, these Observances were in existence and Observed from Creation. THINK ABOUT IT! This makes sense because the first Five Books of the Bible are the Torah. The 613 Observances are contained in these Five Books. Even though the bulk of these Observances are intended only for the Children of Israel, each of us are responsible to observe certain Obligations within The Torah. This is one of the areas religions omit. Religions fail to accurately identify what Obligations human kind is required to observe. We discuss this in the chapter entitled The Revelation of God. In the chapter entitled What Is My Perception Of Judaism we discuss the divisiveness of Religions.

Our Creator did not place us on earth without any direction or form of guidance. We have some responsibilities. We have some obligations. We have some Commands. Objecting to this does not change it.

What about Jonah? Look at Jonah! Jonah's entire message to Nineveh was just six words! Yet because of this six-word message hundreds of thousands of people put on sackcloth and ashes and repented. All that Jonah said was, '*In forty days this city is going to be overthrown.'* In the original language he uses only six words! Yet these six words convey what is necessary to bring about complete change. This teaches us repentance existed. This teaches us people knew how to get real serious with God. They knew how to repent. YET, HOW DID THEY KNOW TO REPENT TO THE LORD GOD? Jonah's only message was, *'In forty days this city is going to be overthrown.'*

In 2 Peter 2:5, Peter said, 'Noach was a preacher of righteousness'. Do you know of where Peter learned this? The Book of Jasher (which was written before Joshua 10.13) states, God told Mesushelach and Noach to proclaim to all the world as follows: *'Thus Says God. Repent of your evil ways and He Will change the decree He Has made against you.'* Sefer HaYashar (Hoboken, NJ: KTAV Publishing House, Inc., 1993) p.16 - A Baptist Pastor gave me my first copy of The Book of Jasher.

Think about it! Noach was born 600 years before

the flood, (See Genesis 7.6). Noach was born in the year 1,056 from Creation. The Bible Says, *'Noah was a* **righteous man perfect in his generations***, and Noah walked with God.'*

Genesis 9.6

אֵלֶּה תוֹלְדֹת נֹחַ נֹחַ אִישׁ צַדִּיק תָּמִים הָיָה בְּדֹרֹתָיו אֶת־הָאֱלֹהִים הִתְהַלֶּךְ־נֹחַ :

The Bible Says Noach was righteous. How is that determined? What is the measuring stick? The Bible Says, Noach was perfect? How is perfection calculated? What formula is used? The Bible Says Noach walked with God. How did Noach reach this high level? These statements are based upon Observances. The Observances are still valid today. They remain the same. No matter how much religions may avoid discussing the Observance they exist and we are required to follow them.

Some Observances are just for women. Some Observances are just for men. Some Observances are for the High Priest. Some are just for the Priests. Some are just for the Levites. Some are just for farmers. Some are just for children. Some are for plants, some for animals, some for mother earth. The point is that there are 613 Observances. Each Observance is a Revelation of God's Light to us. No one Observes all 613 Observances. Yet each of us are Obligated to Observe some of our Creator's Directions for living. How well our world functions or fails to function depends upon each of us doing our righteous part.

The purpose of the Observances is to provide us with direction, to support our good choices and to correct us when we are wrong.

It is written in Sefer Ha Yasher, 'And Enoch lived sixty-five years and he fathered Mesushelach [in 687 FC / From Creation. Enoch walked with God after fathering Mesushelach. He served The Lord, and despised the evil ways of men. The soul of Enoch was wrapped up in the instruction of the Lord, in knowledge and understanding so that he would know all the Ways of the Lord. He wisely withdrew from the sons of men. He lived in seclusion for many years. After serving the Lord and praying before him in his house for many years an Angel of the Lord Called to him. Enoch said, *Here am I.*

The Angel Said, *Rise! Go forth from your house and from the place where you are secluding yourself. Return to humankind and govern them. Teach them in the way they should go and in the correct deeds they should perform.* Enoch rose according to the Word of The Lord Spoken by the Angel. He went forth from his seclusion. He went to the sons of men and taught them the Ways of The Lord. He gathered men together in assemblies and taught them the obligations of the Lord. He published in all places where men dwelt saying, *Where is the man who desires to know the ways of the Lord and good works? Let him come to Enoch.*

The sons of men came and learned from Enoch. Enoch governed over them according to the Word of The Lord. They heard his Word. The

Spirit of God was upon Enoch and he taught all his men the wisdom of God and his ways, and the sons of men served the Lord all the days of Enoch life on earth...'

In the Introduction of this book I mentioned silent areas. Many of the worlds religions do not speak of the times prior to their mystical inception. This is one of the silent areas. How did the world exist and function prior to each religion's inception?

SUMMARY – From Creation there have always been Obligations for us to Observe. The Obligations were established by God, our Creator.

Chapter Three

Good Self Governing

We offer a course at B'nai Noach Torah Institute, LLC called, Prayerful Worship. In this course we Teach short prayerful Words of Worship in Hebrew. We discuss Righteous Individual Responsibility / Good Self Governing! This is possibly the most important Observance of the Bible. Our first parents failed to employ good self governing when dealing with the serpent. Any of us can make the same mistake, Kaw Naw Nah Haw Raw!

Genesis 2.16

And He The Lord God [Creator of everything] Commanded to Adam [And Eve], Saying, from all the trees in the Garden Eat Freely,

Genesis 2.17

But from the Tree of Knowledge of Good and Evil, Do not eat from it, for in the day you eat from it you will die.

There are many ways to describe Good Self Governing. In this specific instance Good Self Governing has to do with being obedient to the Observances of the Lord, *'Do not eat from from the Tree of Knowledge of Good and Evil!* Adam and Eve disobeyed. They ate. All the other trees were freely given to them. Only one specific tree was with held from them. The Lord God did not give them the Tree of Knowledge of Good and Evil. The Lord God did not permit them to eat from the Tree of Knowledge of Good and Evil. When Adam and Eve took just one fruit from the Tree of Knowledge of Good and Evil they stole that fruit from the Lord God. They failed to Observe Good Self Governing! They sinned. This is why good self governing is so very important. When an individual governs his or her self properly that individual is honoring every Obligation of the Bible. To have Good Self Governing skills, sound judgment is necessary.

This is the purpose for *the Torah portion of the Bible.* The Torah Teaches us how to develop sound judgement and how to use good self governing skills. Where else does one learn good self governing skills in the Bible? David wrote:

Psalm 5.8
And as for me, because of Your numerous Kindnesses I will come into Your house to prostrate myself towards Your Holy Sanctuary in awe of You!

Dear Reader David, King of Israel got it! He understood the importance of his individual development of sound judgement and the use of Good Self Governing skills. He understood that even though The Lord God has Commanded each of us to develop sound judgement and the use of Good Self Governing skills. Truly this is an individual responsibility that Government is incapable of legislating. Government punishes violators. The foundation stones for the future, is how each of us will govern ourselves, not how the government will accomplish this.

The point is that if each of us from this second forward, each of us should really try to develop sound judgement and the use of Good Self Governing skills then our world would change immediately. This is what will happen when the Messiah Comes.

We know the story of King Balak. He hired the Prophet Balaam to curse B'nei Yisroel / the Children of Yisroel. He opened his mouth to speak the curse but The Lord changed the Words he said. What did he say? He said,

Numbers 24.5
How goodly are your tents, O Jacob, and your tabernacles, O Israel!

Dear reader Jews say this prayer each morning. Why? It is a reminder to us of the great progress we made from being the last of 70 nations, to being the first nation. Originally our Creator offered each nation His Revelation of Light, The 613 Observances of the Torah. None accepted until He came to the last nation, B'nai Yisroel. We accepted, Avoda Zara 2b.

This is how we became the Holy Nation the sanctified people that Numbers 24.5 speaks.

When the Creator Gave the Torah to Israel, He revealed it. simultaneously in all the 70 languages, so that men of all nations would have a right to the Torah. Shemos Rabba 5.9 - Jewish virtual library .org

The Midrash Says, that Jewish men and women gathered at the foot of Mount Sinai. They were separated. Then they were joined by the millions of unborn Souls of their descendants and the Souls from everyone that would convert to Judaism in all generations. Then together they said, '*All that The Lord Has Spoken, we will do*', Exodus 19.8. Rabbi Moshe Weissman, The Midrash Says The Book Of Shemos (Brooklyn, New York: Benei Yakov Publications 1980), p. 180

Dear Ones, do you follow what I have just

written? Who am I to say you did not stand at the foot of Mount Sinai as one of the millions of unborn souls.

Who am I to judge if your soul was among those unborn souls that would convert at a future date? Who am I to deny any that would come the opportunity to learn when our Creator made the Torah available to all Seventy Languages? So it does not matter if some of you are goofy or if some of you are thought to be crazy. What matters is if you stood before The Lord God at Mount Sinai and promised to Observe all the Commands of the Torah.

If ANYONE DOES ANYTHING to prevent one of these from learning they will answer to The Creator.

Those of you who want to be Jewish acquaint yourselves with this chapter. Do not take a back seat to anyone. Be respectful and polite but do not take a back seat to anyone.

Dear Ones, Any practice that you observe in this life three times becomes like a vow. If one fails to pray three times it's like a vow not to pray. If one studies Torah three times it's like a vow to study The Torah. I am being some what simple, yet, pay attention to the caution. When one sees the beauty of Sabbath it is easy to think that one would always lovingly follow it's path. Be careful! Remember David Wrote,

Psalms 119.105
Your word is a lamp to my feet And a light to my path.

The key Words are lamp and path. A lamp gives light to a trail which is a small path. This means walk on the path only as the Light reveals the way to walk. It is not a six lane freeway!! Take your time. Someday if God is Willing I hope to publish a book on the all the Commands in The Torah portion of the Bible. For anyone who is interested I have a list of the 613 Commands I would be happy to provide. I encourage readers to study the Bible. Research this chapter. Review the references. Feel welcome to ask questions. Contact us at bnti.us.

It is very important for those who are Jewish and those who are not Jewish to understand each have God assigned responsibilities... observances... We each have Commands to follow. Those who are Jewish have a few more Commands to observe than those who are not Jewish.

I know of a Yid (a Jew) who was in financial need. A wealthy man in the community privately gave him several hundred dollars in an envelope. The Yid who received this envelope did not know what was in it. The giver requested that the receiver say one Tehillim / Psalm in behalf of him and his family everyday and that he should ask The Lord to bless him so that he would be financially able to assist other Yidden. The receiver agreed. On other occasions the two would meet in shul / congregation, in shopping places, etc. They were friends and showed great kindness towards each other. Occasionally the giver would assist his poorer brother. After a while the poorer brother did better and did not require assistance. He became wealthy.

Many years later another Yid heard him praying for his dear holy brother and saying a Tehillim for him, his wife and his children. He heard the Yid say Hashem / The Lord bless my holy brother and he named his Hebrew name, etc. The Yid who overheard this prayer knew that the recipient of the prayer was quite wealthy and wondered why this Yid / Jew prayed with such Kavanah / Spiritual Fervency, for him. After observing his prayers for a few weeks his curiosity got the best of him. He had to ask. *'Why do you pray for the very wealthy Jew, his wife and children with such fervency?'*

The answer he received was, *'Many years ago when I was in need this holy brother assisted me. In return for his assistance I promised to say a Tehillim everyday in behalf of him and his family.'*
Upon hearing his answer the curious Yid asked,

'Has he assisted you recently?'

'No, not directly,' was the reply.

The curious Yid questioned, *'So why do you continue to say a Tehillim in his behalf everyday? He hasn't assisted you in years.'*

The Yid responded, *'Because I remember when he did help me.'*

Did this act of appreciation require great self discipline? Was self governing required? I think, perhaps it was. Yet, regardless we see the picture. We observe the commitment.

SUMMARY – As I said previously, there was a time when I would not want the walls of my home to speak of what they heard and saw. Yet, with repentance one reaches the place of good self governing when the walls of ones home glisten with purity and righteousness, Kaw Nah Naw Hah Raw.

Chapter Four

PERCEPTION

When I was a child I remember my father, may he rest in peace, telling this story about perception. My father said there was a very wealthy man and a very poor man that lived in the same village. The wealthy man was successful and very business like. He lived in a fine home in the wealthy part of town. The poor man scraped to make it from day today. He lived in a one room shack at the edge of town. He had an outdoor outhouse and carried water from the creek. He gathered and chopped wood to provide heat for his humble home. His clothes were worn with patches, many sewn on patches. The wealthy man and the poor man knew each other. They attended the same congregation so they often brushed shoulders. The wealthy man was a good individual. He would pass work when he could to the poor man and occasionally help him.

The poor man was a serious student of the Bible. His Bible was worn from use. The poor man would share lessons and stories with the congregation. Occasionally folks would have him over for a meal and to do work they needed done. They would buy a wagon of wood from the poor man. He would deliver and stack it. One morning the wealthy man needed some wood to heat his office so he immediately sent for the poor man. The poor man brought the wood then stayed to chat a short while with the wealthy man. During the conversation the poor man mentioned to the wealthy man that the Creator of the universe revealed to him that He was going to take the most wealthiest man in the village home that very night. They shook hands. The wealthy man paid for the wood and they parted. Immediately the wealthy man called for his accountant, his doctor and his lawyer. He needed to see them immediately. When they arrived the wealthy man was nervous and visibility quite shaken. He was shaking as he passed back and forth. The wealthy man asked his accountant who is the wealthiest man in the village?

His accountant affirmed what he already knew. The accountant said, Sir, you are the most wealthy man in the community hands down. It was like he let out a scream from the painful news. The doctor insisted that the wealthy man sit down. He was concerned about his blood pressure and his heart. He began to take his blood pressure. It was really high. His attorney inquired why he had called for him? The wealthy man said wait, I have some very important business for you to handle. He explained to the three professionals what the poor man said about the wealthiest man in the village, that he would die that evening. Each professional became grievously concerned. They knew the poor man was cautious with his words. He was righteous and walked with God. He was known to pray all night and to often study the Bible all day. They were aware that other things he predicted came true. At that time a knock came at the door. A servant showed a visitor to the room where the wealthy man was being examined by the doctor. He said that he was sorry to learn that he had come down with a sudden illness and that he might not make it through the night. He said that word was out throughout the village. Every member of the village was concerned. As the doctor continued the examination, the wealthy man inquired how much money and assets he would have to divest himself of to be the second wealthiest man in the village. He said, right here and right now, make a list of everything I must rid myself of. The accountant began writing. Then the wealthiest man turned to the attorney and said, I need for you to draw up papers right here and right now that I give this property to this person and this business to that individual and stipulate that even though I give the property away right here and right now that I may purchase each property or business back at anytime during this year for just a dollar per investment. The accountant worked feverishly into the late after noon. The attorney called for his office staff to assist him in completing all the necessary documents. The doctor took the man to the nearest hospital after he had signed all the relinquishment documents in front of a notary. The documents were filed. The doctor spent the entire night with the now second or third wealthiest man in the village. His condition began to improve. He was released from the hospital. His blood pressure was again under control. He returned home. When he arrived home he immediately began inquiring about the wealthiest man in the community. Did he die? No he was told. He is fit as a fiddle. What about this wealthy man and that wealthy person? All were fine. He immediately instructed the servant, *Send for the poor man. I need to speak with him.*

The servant said, I cannot. He died during the night. His funeral is this afternoon.

The wealthy man's perception was that he was going to die. Each of us have perceptions. In this chapter and in the next some of our perceptions will be challenged. PLEASE pay close attention to each reference. And please study them carefully.

What is my perception of Judaism? What has etched my perception of Judaism? How did I develop what I perceive about Judaism. What caused me to formulate the thoughts I have about Jews and The Holy Torah? What is my consciousness of the Hebrew Scriptures? What is my grasp of the Bible? If my perception of Judaism changes how would that impact my desire to be Jewish?

Can you remember what happened exactly three months ago at three in the afternoon? I cannot. We might be able to reconstruct where we were through phone records or receipts, etc., but to know exactly... If we were to go back three years would we be able to say with certainty what the head of our country did? With modern technology we could possibly reconstruct the chronology of one day. Please do this. Pick any day of the year three years ago and try to go back and reconstruct what the head of your country did during a twenty-four hour time period. Using the very best modern technology how much time did this take?

HOW did Matthew, Mark, Luke and John

reconstruct three and half years of Jesus life more than twenty-five years later? Did they design a module to follow? Where and how did they gather their information?

There is a VAST difference from the First Five Books of the Bible in comparison to the Christian Writings. God, the Creator of the universe dictated every Word of the first Five Books of the Bible to Moses. We know the origins of the Torah portion of the Bible. What we don't know is how Matthew, Mark, Luke and John reconstruct three and half years of Jesus life more than twenty-five years later. Let's try another project. Paul advised Titus to '*Avoid foolish questions and genealogies*' in Titus 3:9. The NIV places the date surrounding the authorship of Titus as between 3824 FC to 3827 FC. This means Titus was most likely written before Matthew, Mark, John and possibly Luke. Scholars differ as to when these books were written. The NIV Study Bible New International Version, (Zondervan Bible Publishers, Grand Rapids, Michigan, 1985) Kenneth Barker General Editor, p 1849. **Maybe**

Matthew and Luke should have followed Paul's advice. Can anyone explain to me why Matthew would give Joseph's Genealogy 'IF' Jesus was NOT his son? Christians Teach that Mary, Jesus' Mother was impregnated by The Holy Ghost, Matthew 1:18. I would also like to know why God would choose a married woman?

Matthew 1:19 - '...Joseph Her husband...'

Matthew 1:24 '...his wife.'

Matthew 1:20 What did the Angel say? *'Mary your wife.'* Mary was a married lady.

Let's clear up this espoused business in Matthew 1.18. This was not a Christian marriage. A Christian Pastor did not marry Joseph and Mary. Joseph and Mary were Jewish. We MUST view their marriage in the correct chronological time frame. We must view this from Jewish glasses. Their marriage followed Jewish Observance. The year was 3760 FC.

Let's discuss a frum / strictly observant Jewish Chasanah / wedding. I am presuming Jesus' parents and grand parents were strictly observant even though, from what I read this is questionable. In the year 3,760 FC (From Creation) engagements did not exist in Judaism. This is a more recent development. Then there were three ways to take a wife. To a degree, a wife is looked upon as property. A wife is not owned like property. Yet, a wife is the possession of her husband. The Torah Teaches 'a man לקח Lih Qah Ach takes a wife'.

Genesis 12.19

לָמָה אָמַרְתָּ אֲחֹתִי הִוא וָאֶקַּח אֹתָהּ לִי
לְאִשָּׁה וְעַתָּה הִנֵּה אִשְׁתְּךָ קַח וָלֵךְ׃

Why did you say, She is my sister? so I might have **taken her for my wife**; now therefore behold your wife, take her, and go your way.

Genesis 24.1-4

וְאַבְרָהָם זָקֵן בָּא בַּיָּמִים וַיהוָה בֵּרַךְ אֶת־אַבְרָהָם בַּכֹּל: וַיֹּאמֶר אַבְרָהָם אֶל־עַבְדּוֹ זְקַן בֵּיתוֹ הַמֹּשֵׁל בְּכָל־אֲשֶׁר־לוֹ שִׂים־נָא יָדְךָ תַּחַת יְרֵכִי: וְאַשְׁבִּיעֲךָ בַּיהוָה אֱלֹהֵי הַשָּׁמַיִם וֵאלֹהֵי הָאָרֶץ אֲשֶׁר לֹא־תִ**קַּח** אִשָּׁה לִבְנִי מִבְּנוֹת הַכְּנַעֲנִי אֲשֶׁר אָנֹכִי יוֹשֵׁב בְּקִרְבּוֹ: כִּי אֶל־אַרְצִי וְאֶל־מוֹלַדְתִּי תֵּלֵךְ וְ**לָקַחְתָּ** אִשָּׁה לִבְנִי לְיִצְחָק:

And Abraham was old, and well advanced in age; and the Lord had blessed Abraham in all things. And Abraham said to the oldest servant of his house, who ruled over all that he had, Put, I beg you, your hand under my thigh; And I will make you swear by The Lord, The God of Heaven, and The God of the earth, that **you shall not** לקח **take a wife** for my son of the daughters of the Canaanites, among whom I live; But you shall go to my country, and to my family, and לקח **take a** wife for my son Isaac.

The Strong's reference number is 3947. I understand this is confusing. Pay attention only to the black Hebrew Letters. The Word לקח Lih Qah Ach means to take a wife. One acquires a wife by taking her. She may refuse then the man is prohibited from taking her. If the Wife agrees to be taken this is accomplished through one of three methods.

1. A wife may be acquired through money or an item of value like a ring.
2. A wife may be acquired through a written agreement.
3. A wife may be acquired through a physical relationship.

Regardless, this must be accomplished in the presence of two witnesses. Two male witnesses above the age of twelve must observe the man or his agent give money or and item of value for his wife. The wife or her agent must acknowledge her willingness to be taken. Two male witnesses above the age of twelve must sign the written agreement. At this point they are married! This means Mary could simply no longer be engaged or espoused. Mary could not just give Joseph back his money or article of value. Why? They were married. At this point Mary was Joseph's wife and Joseph was Mary's husband. For either to separate this would require a Jewish get, i.e. a Jewish divorce.

This is very significant. Why? God, the Creator of all would not impregnate Mary for any reason, and even more important God would not take another man's wife and impregnate her.

Later two male witnesses above the age of twelve must observe the man and woman enter the bedroom chamber. They stand guard in view of the door. After the marriage relationship is consummated and the couple exits the room the witnesses collect the marriage cloth from the bed. The blood on the marriage cloth is proof of the wife's virginity. It is given tp her father.

Now, how are individuals who are not Jewish going to know this process. How are you going to know I omitted several details? The point is Christians know nothing about the parents of Joseph and Mary. We know two names. Why did Matthew, Mark, Luke and John omit the important background on the parents of Joseph and Mary? We know that Matthew 1:15,16 says that Jacob is the father of Joseph. We know that Luke 3.23,24 says, Heli was the father of Joseph. Christians have not resolved the issues with Jesus genealogy. Annius of Viterbo at the end of the 15th century suggested Matthew's genealogy was that of Joseph and Luke's genealogy was that of Mary. The Pulpit Commentary Volume 22 Epistles of Peter, John and Jude. The Revelation (Grand Rapids, Michigan, Wm. B. Eerdmans Publishing Company, reprint 1975) p70,71.

The facts are that the genealogies do not match. Even if both genealogies were supposed to be Joseph's what does this prove. Again, Christians teach the Holy Ghost was Jesus' father. Why then put either of these genealogies in the

Christian Writings. What is the purpose? What perception does this give? What does this clarify? How is this helpful? What are we supposed to gain from this? We possibly know the name of Joseph's father. He may have two names. We don't know. We may know the name of Mary's father.

Try comparing the two genealogies. It takes time. It is difficult. Compare the genealogies to 1Chronicles 1.27 to 3.19. The Christian Writings. omits 4 important genealogies. What is even more amazing is that all either Matthew or John needed to do was to obtain a copy of Chronicles and copy it into their writings. Why didn't they do this?

We know that Jesus as an **'adopted son'** cannot come from the line of Matthew. IT DISQUALIFIES JESUS from ascending the Throne of David!! Matthew clearly says the Holy Ghost was Jesus father. He was not from the linage of Joseph according to Matthew, Mary was impregnated from the seed of the Holy Ghost. It was NOT from the seed of Joseph according to Matthew!

We know that regardless of whose genealogy Luke is providing IT DISQUALIFIES JESUS from ascending the Throne of David!! WHY? Look at Luke 3.31. The genealogy of Luke says Jesus genealogy was through Nathan the son of David. See 1 Chronicles 3.5. Why is this significant? Nathan's mother is Bathshua and his father is David. However, 2 Samuel informs us that the lineage of Messiah MUST be a descendant of David through his son Solomon.

2 Samuel 7.12,13

And when your days shall be fulfilled, and you sleep with your fathers, I will set up your seed after you, which shall proceed out of your bowels, and I will establish his kingdom. ***He shall build an House for My Name, and I will establish the throne of his kingdom for ever.***

Dear Reader Nathan did NOT build the house, the Holy Temple, Solomon did. Nathan was

NEVER King! Solomon was. Jesus cannot be the Messiah. Now, I do not believe that Jesus is God. I do not believe the Holy Ghost impregnated Mary. Why?

WHAT DO WE KNOW ABOUT MARY'S PARENTS? WE DO KNOW THE PARENTS OF JOSEPH AND MARY ARE ABSENT. That is a serious problem. Why?

The Jewish Community that Joseph's parents lived in knew the marriage was not consummated. The Jewish Community that Mary's parents lived in knew the marriage was not consummated. Ask yourself this question. What would you do when you could see your married daughter was six months along? Biblically what would you do? Do you really believe the Creator of the universe would place a twelve year old bride in this position? I do not!

Would Mary's noticeable pregnancy appear wrong to her parents? Would Mary's noticeable pregnancy appear wrong to the Jewish

Community where her family lived? Would it seem odd that Mary did not visit the Community Mikvah each month after her period? Would Mary's noticeable pregnancy appear wrong to her husband?

Why was Joseph informed of his wife's pregnancy only after it was noticeable?

How does this appear? Does this have the appearance of wrong? Does this have the appearance of evil?

Betrothal was much more to the Semitic races. Betrothal was binding as marriage. The Pulpit Commentary Volume 22 Epistles of Peter, John and Jude. The Revelation (Grand Rapids, Michigan, Wm. B. Eerdmans Publishing Company, reprint 1975) p5

Time and again the Gospel writers make comments that cannot be substantiated. Here is one for example:

Matthew 28.11

Now when they were going, behold, some of the watch came into the city and told the chief priests all the things that were done. And when they were assembled with the elders and had taken counsel they gave large sums of money to the soldiers saying, ye shall say, His disciples came by night ...

Matthew is making strong accusations. They may be true. They maybe false. Many Christians believe these accusations. That is their choice. Yet, Matthew writes of these events like they are fact. He is quoting an unnamed source. The Torah requires witnesses.

How about the story of legion in Mark 5. Mark writes that a man was possessed with unclean spirits. Jesus allegedly cast these unclean spirits out of the man and sends them into a large herd of swine. Thousands of swine charge down a steep cliff and into the sea and drowned.

How would you like to be the owner of the swine? If this story were true it would seem like Jesus would owe the owner damages for the swine. This would be a significant loss. How is it that this story comes out of nowhere, then disappears. Little is said about the owners of the swine. Christians read this story like it is matter of fact. Yet history does not support this story. There are many claims in the Christian Writings like this. What about the story of five loaves and two fish? Allegedly Jesus feeds five thousand men plus women and children. Where do we read of these events in history? Ask yourself, would each of these three stories be significant news events? Would historians document them? Would records exist? Outside of Josephus little is said.

Dear reader you may think that I have discredited the Christian Scriptures. Yet, everything I shared was true. I have not smeared or blackened Christianity. Everything is in plain sight. Nothing has been twisted or misrepresented. Take the time to study this chapter. Let it soak in. I understand how upsetting this may be for you.

Yet, do you want to know the truth? Now on the other hand this chapter should have answered many questions. I asked the question at the beginning of this chapter, If my perception of Judaism changes, how would that impact my desire to be Jewish?

SUMMARY - For the past twenty pages we have been discussing perception. How is God perceived if He impregnated a twelve year old girl who was married placing her life in jeopardy? How does Joseph perceive what is to have allegedly happened to his wife? How is this Outspoken Young Jewish Rabbi perceived if he really did cast thousands of unclean spirits out of a man and into a herd of swine which resulted in their deaths? How is the news perceived that shows it is impossible for Jesus to be the Messiah because his genealogy prohibits this? Would you like to be Jewish? At this point in the book some readers will feel devastated. You maybe wondering what am I going to do from here? Please stay with us. We are going to learn what to do and where to go from here.

Chapter Five

Disinformation

The Ninth Concept Teaches our present Torah portion of the Bible is eternal.

God Will Never amend nor exchange His Torah for another, for all eternity.

Dear Reader there is a great deal of disinformation written and spoken about the Hebrew Scriptures. We could also call it propaganda. It is biased, misleading and a lie. I think a good many of us enjoy a little fundamental misleading of others from time to time. Many individuals are bewildered, confused, puzzled, baffled, mystified, befuddled and confused about what the Hebrew Scriptures Teach. This chapter will help to clarify what the Covenant between God and the Jewish people is and how disoriented Christianity is on this subject.

As we begin our study, an area that will be confusing is the chapter and verse numbering between the Hebrew Scriptures and the English Bible. Christians did this. The Hebrew Scriptures are in scrolls without numbers for chapters or verses. The Greeks changed all the names of the books for the Hebrew Scriptures and put in place there own numbering system about two thousand years ago. It's a little like the Genealogy of Jesus in Matthew and Luke. The genealogy goes in two different directions. It is confusing. When the Hebrew Scriptures and the English Bible don't always match verse by verse or chapter by chapter this is also confusing. In this book I follow the numbering system the Greeks put into place for the Hebrew Scriptures.

When I was younger during the summers I enjoyed being a Colorado Historical Society Tour Guide up in the mountains. I gave hard rock mine tours and taught steam train history for our area. We would take guests about five hundred feet back into an old silver mine. A guide gives the same tour over and over day in and day out. I led over a thousand tours in this mine. I was very good. One guide, may he rest in peace, constantly exaggerated on his tour. The people loved him. I think they realized he was really going out on a limb with some of his stories. The two of us were very entertaining. One year I began after July fourth. By then I was a relic. This other guide told so many stories about me that new employees practically bowed in front of me when I returned. They came to me to inquire if the stories they heard were true. I would ask them to tell me the story. For the most part they were true with some embellishment. I would also tell stories about this other guide. He had a good heart. Several times a year the two of us would get together around a camp fire to spin tales. If you could get the two of us together around a camp fire with a little something to warm us we would light up the night. You would laugh yourself silly. He would tell stories about me and I would tell stories about him. Some of my stories were like his. They were way out there on a limb. I was famous for the story of One Eyed One Armed Jack. He was famous for the Hanging

Tree. We were both instructed to stop telling these stories. On the last tour of the year I was famous for holding the steam train up for about an hour and a half. I gave the longest tour of the year. Both of us were back in the hard rock mine at different times when slides and cave ins happened. It was scarey and interesting. The roughest looking guests knew how to pray. It would not take too many falling rocks to sober a drunk.

I really liked to interact with the guests. On a good day I would learn the name of almost every guest in the tour. That would be twenty to thirty five people. It was a challenge and it was fun. It drew people into the tour. I looked like a miner with a gray beard hard hat and light. Guest were always wanting to take pictures with me. It made them feel a part of everything. Very few knew who I really was. It was so much fun to have New York Chasidim on a tour. One year there was this disagreement on the steam train between the Engineer and 87 Israelis. The Israelis claimed they paid for the Historic mine tour. However their booking agent at the train station made a mistake. The engineer would not let the Israelis off the train and the Israelis would not let the train move. They called for me. Once the Israelis told me they paid for the Historic mine tour I was required to take their word. I told the engineer regardless if they had tickets or not we were going to do the mine tour. All of them were on my tour. They were all taking pictures with me. They were shocked I was wearing my kippah and tzitzit. Later we learned that I made the right decision. The tour <u>was</u> paid for.

One year there was this large Texan. He was tall, broad and heavy. I would say somewhere around 6' 8" tall and around 360 pounds. He had a large straw cowboy hat, shirt, blue jeans and a huge cowboy belt buckle. There was this tiny petite lady with him. They acted like husband and wife. They seemed like a nice couple. I could not resist. It was time for some disinformation. A guide knows when he / she has had a great tour and has the guests in the palm of his / her hand. Such was the case on this tour. We had just exited the mine. The tour was concluding. My cell phone began ringing. This was the opportunity I had been looking for. For whatever reason I got the strongest impression that this huge burly fellow just didn't like housework. I got the impression that he thought this was women's work. Being the Teacher I am, I made it impossible to resist. I answered my cell phone. It was a short call. All the guests were still watching and listening to my conversation. They did not know that the conversation was over. There was no one on the other end. The phone was blank. At that exact time I said, Yes dear, in a louder voice, What? You want me to do a load of laundry when I get home after work to night. Yes mam. I will. What? After I start the wash you want me to do the bathrooms. O.K. O.K. I will. What? Be careful to extra scrub the... O.K. Honey, I have to go. I have guests... What ? Iron your blouse. O.K but that is....

About that time I saw the tiny petit woman take her elbow and give her husband a serious poke in the ribs... It was so funny. It was all I could do to keep a straight face. Dear Reader what I just described is disinformation. Yes, I was having some fun. No harm was done. Yet I was misleading.

In the fourth chapter of this book I shared some very important information about Jesus. The information is true. Do you think your Pastor, Priest or Teacher may know some or all of this information? I think some may. Share what I wrote in chapter four with them. Watch their reaction. Then judge for yourself, are they seeking Truth or Religion. What I shared in chapter four is completely referenced. If you are a Christian who believes in Jesus, chapter four will possibly anger you. Yet, it is true. What you are about to read in this chapter is also true. I will reference everything. It will not make it easy if you are rocking and reeling from the revelations in chapter four.

There has been an on going campaign to discredit *the Torah portion of the Bible* for around 1,821 years. The term 'Old Testament' began appearing in Christian writing in 3948 FC. Holman writes that the term Old Testament implies a New Testament. Holman Bible Dictionary, (Holman Bible Publishers, Nashville, Tennessee 1991) p 185

Quote #1 - **Recently a Christian wrote,** *'I am ready to "give up" OT teachings,* for teaching, because t**hey have nothing to do with the gentiles, Jesus FULFILLED the prophecies...** Christians who actually read the NT...will tell you that Jesus specifically states that He is the fulfillment of the OT...'

Quote #2 - Another writer states, 'Fulfillment means that [Jesus] has completed the old and brought it to its full expression in the new... **The Old Testament authors foresaw a time of fulfillment...** Fulfillment of the Old in the New underscores the severity of the justice of God in the Old Testament.'

Quote #3 - Another writes, **Critics of the Bible often cite Old Testament instances of slavery,** *violence against homosexuals, wiping out nations, etc., as evidence of a morally inadequate set of rules.* They... ask why... Christians don't follow these **"barbaric" teachings** today. The reason... is because **the Old Covenantal system, that involved such harsh punishments, has been done away with.** We are under a new covenant... Jesus said in Luke 22:20, This cup which is poured out for you is the new covenant in My blood.

This new covenant was prophesied in the Old Testament in Jeremiah 31.31. [English Scriptures] Behold, days are coming, declares the Lord, when **I will make a new covenant with the house of Israel and with the house of Judah.**

Many years before returning to Judaism I attended a New Testament Church. They carried New Testaments. They taught out of the New Testament. The Pastor considered himself a Pauline Christian. He was a loving man. Yet he rejected the Hebrew Scriptures. They were old, fulfilled and done away with.

Dear Reader there are vast misunderstandings, enormous disinformation and outlandish lies that pillar these four quotes. The individuals that write these quotes are hardened in their belief. Only powerful revelation from our Creator will change these beliefs. You are not among this group. These are dedicated God fearing people who really have strong desires to honor and follow the Christian Scriptures. Their beliefs are strongly held and deeply rooted. Even though you are not among these we are going to discuss one of the important concepts of Judaism, **God Will Never amend nor exchange His Torah for another, for all eternity.**

Individuals who believe this way go back over 18 centuries. Look at the language, *"barbaric" teachings.* **This is strong language.** *They believe they are rescuing the world from slavery, violence against homosexuals and wiping out nations. They believe and teach that the Hebrew Scriptures are a morally inadequate set of rules.*

It is difficult to reach folks like these. They believe Jews cannot recognize Jesus as the Messiah because our eyes are blinded. Yet most of these individuals cannot read or write three Words in Hebrew. These very strong feelings have to do with how we are raised. They have to do with our strong commitment to God.

Years ago my first wife was going to need surgery. We were separated and would eventually get divorced. I asked her if she had transportation to the hospital. She said, *Yes.*
I asked again, *Are you sure?*
Again, she said, *Yes,* while nodding her head in affirmation.
I asked her 'Would you like for me to be there during your surgery?' she said, *No.* I said, *O.K. I am going to go ahead and schedule some business appointments...* Around eight AM the next morning my phone began ringing. It was my first wife. She needed me to come take her to the hospital for the surgery. I said, O.K. Then began calling clients to cancel appointments. We lived about eighteen miles apart. I arrived a little late.

Her mother was understandably disappointed. They were waiting. I parked my old truck. Got her car keys. Immediately they got into her car. We left for the hospital. We arrived possibly a little late. She was taken into surgery. The surgery went well, thank God. During the surgery I sat outside in the waiting room with my former mother-in-law. She is a nice lady. She strongly believes in God. She tries to be a dedicated Christian. She had been very good to her daughters, grand children and her great grand children. She tried to be a good mother-in-law.

We were sitting in the waiting room. I was silently praying that the surgery would be successful. I brought along a book that was very special to me. It was the Book of Psalms. However the outside said, The Metsudah Tehillim. The title was repeated in smaller Hebrew Block Letters. The printing was on what most English readers would call the back cover. I read Psalms 20 then prayed some more then read Psalms 20 again. My mother-in-law was very nervous. She would get up select a magazine then sit down. Then

again in a few minutes get up select another magazine and sit down, etc. This is understandable. She was very concerned for her daughter. I thought maybe the psalms would comfort her. I handed her my Book of Psalms. She took it then asked, What is this?
I responded this, is the Book of Psalms. It's and Linear of Hebrew and English.
She asked something like, Is this one of those Jewish things?
I said, it's the Psalms in English and Hebrew. It the same as the book of Psalms in your Bible. Then she took a quick glance then sat it down like a hot pan. She had a look that felt like my hands are burned. Don't give me that thing. She wasn't hateful. She was taken off guard.

Thank God! The surgery was a success.

Dear readers, my father offered my former spouse a large sum of money if she would take his grandsons and leave the state. His opinion was I was too educated. Yet, after my father passed from this life, on that very night he came to my bedside to apologize for how he treated me. I forgave him.

I have a brother who loves me but will not say my name Akiva. I enquire how my brother's congregations are doing. For the most part they do not want to know anything about Judaism. One brother has banned me from speaking with his children or wife about the Torah or Judaism. So dear reader I have some experience with this mind set.

Christians maintain that the doctrine supporting the New Writings comes from Jeremiah 31.30. They are mistaken. There is a difference in saying the Words New Covenant from that of developing a New Covenant Doctrine. An entire religion has been spun off this Verse.

Jeremiah 31.30 / Jeremiah 31.31 (English)

הִנֵּה יָמִים בָּאִים נְאֻם־יְהוָה וְכָרַתִּי
אֶת־בֵּית יִשְׂרָאֵל וְאֶת־בֵּית יְהוּדָה
בְּרִית חֲדָשָׁה:

Behold days are coming, Says The Lord, I will Make everything from Aleph to Tav with the House of Israel and everything from Aleph to Tav with the House of Yehudah, a new covenant.

Jeremiah is writing that the Lord is going to make a new Covenant – NOT A NEW TORAH - . The present covenant is in the flesh of our foreskin. The New Covenant will be between the House of ISRAEL and the House of YEHUDAH. The covenant will have nothing to do with Christians or Jesus.

Jeremiah 31.31 / Jeremiah 31.32 (English)

לֹא כַבְּרִית אֲשֶׁר כָּרַתִּי אֶת־אֲבוֹתָם בְּיוֹם הֶחֱזִיקִי
בְיָדָם לְהוֹצִיאָם מֵאֶרֶץ מִצְרָיִם אֲשֶׁר־הֵמָּה הֵפֵרוּ
אֶת־בְּרִיתִי וְאָנֹכִי בָּעַלְתִּי בָם נְאֻם־יְהוָה:

Not like the covenant made from Aleph to Tav with the fathers in the day I strengthen their hand to come out from the land of Egypt. They broke Everything from Aleph to Tav of that Covenant, although I was a husband to them, says the Lord.

Exodus 12.43,44
And the Lord said to Moses and Aaron, This is the ordinance of the passover: No alien shall eat thereof: However when every man's servant is bought for money, then you shall circumcise him, then shall he eat thereof. A foreigner and an hired servant shall not eat thereof.

Exodus 12.48
And when a proselyte shall sojourn with you, and will keep the Passover to the Lord, **let all his males be circumcised**, *and then let him come near and keep it; and he shall be as one who is born in the land;* **for no uncircumcised person shall eat of it.**

The Midrash Teaches when the Israelites saw

that the uncircumcised were disqualified from eating the Passover, they arose with the least possible delay and circumcised all their servants and sons and all those who [subsequently] went out with them...

[Moses Said,] Unless the seal of Abraham is inscribed on your flesh, you cannot taste thereof. Thereupon all those who had been born in Egypt were immediately circumcised... Thereupon they immediately offered themselves for circumcision, and the blood of the Passover mingled with that of circumcision. Shemot Rabba 19.4,5

What is the point? Jeremiah Says, *Not like the covenant made from Aleph to Tav with the fathers in the day I strengthen their hand to come out from the land of Egypt.*

This Teaches us that all the men who were Jewish, the men who were servants of Jews that were bought with money and converts to Judaism each had to enter into the covenant of Avraham. They did this before they left Egypt.

They did this before the Passover offering. Jeremiah is making reference to this covenant.

Jeremiah 31.32 / Jeremiah 31.33 (English)

כִּי זֹאת הַבְּרִית אֲשֶׁר אֶכְרֹת אֶת־בֵּית יִשְׂרָאֵל אַחֲרֵי הַיָּמִים הָהֵם נְאֻם־יְהֹוָה נָתַתִּי **אֶת־תּוֹרָתִי** בְּקִרְבָּם וְעַל־לִבָּם אֶכְתְּבֶנָּה וְהָיִיתִי לָהֶם לֵאלֹהִים וְהֵמָּה יִהְיוּ־לִי לְעָם:

For this, the covenant that I make, everything from the Aleph to the Tav with the House of Israel after those days, Says The Lord, I will bestow everything from the Letter Aleph to the Letter Tav of My Torah within them, and on their hearts I will write it, and I will be within them as [a revelation of] God and they will be to Me a nation.

At this time *the written Torah portion* of the Bible that we presently have will be placed within the heart, i.e. soul, mind of the House of Israel. It will be a little like the GPS system that guides us from one location to another. The House of Israel will always know the Obligations to the Lord and how to correctly decipher them.

There is nothing in Jeremiah that talks about Christians. All the discussion is to the House of Israel and the House of Yehudah. The Teachings that Christians claim to be fulfilled and done away with are the very Teachings that God places within the Jewish people and writes upon their heart. God's Covenant with the Jewish people is circumcision. That is not the Torah! They are NOT the same. A man cannot enter into Judaism without being circumcised. Yet, ALL OF US are guided by the Obligations by the Observances in the Torah. That NEVER changes. The cut agreement between the House of Israel will change from being one on the male organ to being one on the Jewish soul. The Torah will remain the same. The very beautiful part of this prophecy is

Jeremiah 31.33 / Jeremiah 31.34 (English)
And they shall teach no more every man his neighbor, and every man his brother, saying, Know the Lord: for they shall all know me, from the least of them unto the greatest of them, Says the Lord: for I will forgive their iniquity, and I will

remember their sin no more.

Now we are going to review a divisive theme that has been woven into religious doctrinal fabric for about eighteen hundreds of years. The teaching is false and misleading. The doctrine is not only false it is heinous!!

Ask any reasonable person who fears God and loves the Bible if Psalms 23 is important to them. Ask them, do you receive comfort from the Psalms? Most of us do.

Dear Reader where are the prophecies regarding the end of days found? Where are the prophecies regarding Moshiach / Messiah found? Where is EVERY instruction regarding tithing found? Where are the battles of Armageddon found? Where is the seventy weeks discussed? The answer is in the Hebrew Scriptures.

This past Sabbath Revi, my wife, and I discussed the etymology of 'the New Testament.' and the etymology of the 'Old Testament'. As a side note:

For those who do not know Revi came to B'nai Noach Torah Institute, LLC as a classmate. Immediately she stood out as exceptional student. Revi learned with us for several years. She was one of those top of the class kind of students. We have had quite a few, thank God!! Exceptional students draw the attention of their Teachers. Every Teacher at our institute recolonized Revi's uniqueness. The top students have such self motivation to learn. It is wonderful! There is no way to describe this hunger for learning. I have had students fly in from around the world just to sit down for a few hours and learn together. IT IS AWSOME! This is not an everyday event. Yet, students e-mail us about their travel plans and want to stop by to learn. Having said this, Revi never came to learn with us.

During those years I was always looking for voluntary research assistances. Teaching six full time courses each week requires assistance. It was so difficult. I asked Revi if she would consider being one of my research assistants and she replied yes. I was immediately impressed by her research. It was excellent. Revi understood what it meant to reference theological studies, thank God!! After serving as my research assistant for several years Revi became a Teacher at B'nai Noach Torah Institute, LLC.

She was assigned just one class. Eventually that developed into several classes.

I scheduled a Teacher conference in St Louis, Missouri close to where Revi lived. AMAZING! She attended. After years of teaching together we finally met. It was an amazing meeting. That is another story. Months later we were married. Revi, my wife is still my research assistant, thank God Kaw Naw Nah Haw Raw! Revi is the only individual I know that may have more Seforim than I have. The two of us are a library!

Back to the subject....

This past Sabbath when we were having this

discussion about the etymology of 'the New Testament' and the etymology of the 'Old Testament'. Revi went into our library and pulled a few books.

We are going to do a little refocusing now... As stated above, there has been this on going campaign to discredit *the Torah portion* of the Bible for around 1,821 years. The term 'Old Testament' began appearing in Christian writings in 3948 FC. This implies a New Testament. There has been this struggle of sorts. The Jewish scholars say established and reliable. Christian scholars say 'Old'. We have to get away from this. It is NOT pleasing to our Creator.

In Judaism we are careful to protect our writings. Dr. Norman L. Geishler, Dr. William E. Nix, authors of <u>A General Introduction to the Bible</u> note this in their discussions on the Old Testament Canon as does Dr. Josh McDowell in his book <u>Evidence that Demands A Verdict</u>. They both discuss the amazing reliability of the Hebrew Scriptures. This brings us to when Jesus' followers were trying to introduce their writings into the Jewish synagogues. The writings were rejected. They were branded as new and unreliable. So, on the one hand we have Christians calling the Hebrew Scriptures old, fulfilled and out dated. On the other hand we have cautious Jews who guard the writings of the Hebrew Scriptures as reliable and well founded. They are extremely concerned that none of these writings make it into the Hebrew Scriptures. What would you do?

I am offended when someone says, Old Testament to me! There is nothing 'OLD' about the Hebrew Scriptures!! Dear Reader do you see what religion has done? Do you see the divisiveness of the Terms 'Old Testament' and 'New Testament' that began working there way into religious doctrine eighteen hundred years ago? The Bible is not about Old or New. Religion is not about Old and New. We are about to see the falseness of the religious doctrines that teach the Hebrew Scriptures are fulfilled and done away with.

Matthew 5:19

Whosoever therefore shall break one of these least [Observances], and shall teach men so, he shall be called the least in the kingdom of heaven: but whosoever shall do and teach them, the same shall be called great in the kingdom of heaven. **Who said this?**

Matthew 19:17

...If you want to enter into life, keep the [Observances]. **Who said this?**

Now one may argue that Jesus was speaking to a Jewish following when he made these comments, however, Matthew could have made this distinction but he did not. Matthew wrote this book more than 25 years after Paul wrote other books of the Christian Writings. Matthew had the opportunity as did Mark and Luke to say Jesus intended these teachings, from the Torah, to be only for Jewish followers, but they did not make that distinction.

What Jesus is reported to have said may seem to differ with Paul's Teaching. They do! Paul taught a great deal about grace. For the most part, the gospels were all written after most of Paul's writings. This being the situation, one must consider why the gospels were written. One could easily make the argument, that in part it was to dispel some of what Paul taught about grace.

Dear reader, you are looking for answers. Is it possible that the answers you seek cannot be found within the boundaries you are looking? I know, if you want to be Jewish, the answers you seek are in the Hebrew Scriptures! Jesus clearly supports the Observances of the Torah. Paul wavers back and forth. We will discuss Paul in Chapter Seven.

Paul wrote to Timothy saying,
2 Timothy 2:16.
'All Scripture is given by inspiration of God and is profitable for doctrine, for reproof for correction, for instruction in righteousness,'

When did Paul write these words? At the time Paul wrote 2Timothy 2.16 the Christian Writings did not exist. Did you know that the words 'it is written' in the Christian Writings occurs over seventy-five times. The term Scripture occurs thirty times in the Christian Writings. The term Scriptures occurs over twenty times in the Christian Writings. Each of these, i.e 'Scriptures', 'Scripture', and 'It is written' are in reference ONLY to The Hebrew Scriptures. Again, the Christian Writings did not exist when they were written.

Dear Reader have you considered what David wrote?

Psalms 19.7 - 11
'The Torah of the Lord is Perfect, reviving the soul; the testimony of the Lord is sure, Making wise the simple. The Statutes of the Lord are right, rejoicing the heart; the Commandment of the Lord is pure, enlightening the eyes. The fear of the Lord is clean, enduring for ever; the Judgments of the Lord are true and righteous

altogether. <u>More to be desired are they than gold, even very fine gold; sweeter also than honey and the honeycomb. Moreover by them is your servant warned; and in keeping of them there is great reward</u>.

What sense does it make for Catholics and Christians to teach that the Perfect Torah of the Lord is done away with? Why would Christians say the Hebrew Scriptures are done away with when Jesus says, '...*if you want to enter into life, keep the Commandments?' Again,* The Christian Scriptures quotes the Words, 'it is written' over 75 times, the Word, 'Scripture' over 30 times and the Word 'Scriptures' over 20 times? At the time of their chronological writing each were making reference to the Hebrew Scriptures. None of these Verses were making reference to the Christian writings. My writings are not anti Catholic or Christian. I am just saying, people get real. Think about what you say you believe.

Dear Reader if one actually believed that the Hebrew Scriptures were done away, what would be the value of Psalm 23 or Psalm 91? Why study the prophecies of Isaiah and other Books? If this were the situation why do Christians bind the Hebrew Scriptures with the Christian Bible? Why do they attach that which they claim to be 'OLD,' and fulfilled and done away with to that which they call 'NEW' and prophetic? It is beyond the time to change mistakes of the past. I think it is better to use appropriate respectful terms like The Hebrew Scriptures and The Christian Bible.

Deuteronomy 29.29
The secret things belong to the Lord our God; but those things which are revealed belong to us and to our children forever, that we may do all the words of this Torah.

Psalm 119.89
For ever, O Lord, your Word is fixed in Heaven.

Psalm 119.44
I shall keep your Torah continually for ever and ever.

The point is, as this chapter has demonstrated, the Hebrew Scriptures are very important. The Hebrew Scriptures are very much alive and endure 'FOREVER'. The Word Torah occurs over 200 times in the Hebrew Scriptures. Why do translators write 'Law' instead of Torah?
Solomon wrote,

Hear, children, the instruction of a father, and attend to know understanding. For I give you a good doctrine, do not forsake my Torah, Proverbs 4.1,2.

Deuteronomy 30.4

If you shall listen to the voice of the Lord your God, to keep his commandments and his statutes which are written in this book of the Torah, and if you turn to the Lord your God with all your heart, and with all your soul.

Joshua 23.6

Be you therefore very courageous to keep and to do all that is written in the Book of the Torah of

Moses, that you should not turn aside from the right hand or from the left;

Psalms 119.34

Give me understanding, and I shall keep your Torah; I shall observe it with my whole heart.

There is a special message in Luke 24:44,45. Jesus delivers this message hours before his death. Perhaps it was his final message. *And he said unto them, These are the words which I spake unto you, while I was yet with you, that all things must be fulfilled, which are written in* **the law of Moses**, *and in* **the prophets,** *and in* **the psalms,** *concerning me. Then opened he their understanding, that they might understand* **the scriptures...**

The Law of Moses is the תורה Torah.

The Prophets is the נביאים Nevi'im.

The Psalms is from כתובים the Writings.

This spells תנכ or תנך Tanakh. What is Tanakh?

Tanakh is an acrostic that Spells the three portions of the Hebrew Scriptures that Jesus opened his disciples understanding to.

the תורה Torah, נביאים the Prophets, and כתובים the Writings. The Hebrew Scriptures are divided into one of these three groups. We call the Hebrew Scriptures תנך Tanakh. They are the Letters ת Tav נ Nun and כ Chof. The Letter כ Chof changes from a normal Letter to a final Letter ך Chof when it is at the end of a Word. The Gematria of Tanakh is 470. Dr. Josh McDow says, [This is Jesus'] witness to the [Hebrew Scriptures] Canon. Dr. Josh McDowell Evidence that Demands A Verdict (Campus Crusade 14th printing July 1977) p 35

What does God want? God wants us to observe all the words of his Torah. God wants us to acknowledge that the Torah is alive and well and will continue forever. **God Will Never amend nor**

exchange His Torah for another, for all eternity.

SUMMARY - Religions of the world MUST STOP using painful hurtful terms in communication. <u>Terms</u> like Old Testament and New Testament are NOT INSPIRED BY GOD and not a part of the Inspiration of The Bible!! They reflect the prejudice of men and religions. They should not be the heading one sees first in Books written to reflect truth and righteousness. Terms like Hebrew Scriptures, Christian Writings or Christian Bible are preferred. Terms like Old and New lack truthfulness. We need to be truthful. We need to come together. There is no contest here. We love God and want to serve him. Let's do so in a way that produces positive results. It is far beyond the time to change mistakes of the past. So let's do it.

Chapter Six

613 Observances

The Seventh Concept Teaches our *present Torah portion* of the Bible was written by one very educated man with Vision.

In Israel none like Moses arose again. He is a prophet who clearly perceived His Vision Given by The Lord God.

In this chapter we want our Reader to be aware of the 613 Observances and the writer. In the Next chapter we will actually discuss Moses and the Inspiration of his Vision.

The Revelation of God to humankind is through the 613 Commandments / Observances. I discuss this in my book entitled: MYSTERIOUS SIGNS Of The Torah Revealed IN GENESIS in chapter one. Pick it up! Get a copy. The first chapter is worth the entire price of the book.

We are about to open the doors of revelation to the 613 Observances. The 613 Commands were given exclusively to the Children of Israel on Mount Sinai. This makes sense because the first Five Books of the Bible are chronological. The 613 Observances are contained in them. However to a degree each of us are responsible to Observe some portions of the Torah. As I have already stated, some Commands are just for B'nei Yisroel / The Children of Israel. Other Commands are for every human on this earth. Some Commands are just for women. Some Commands are just for men. Some Commands are for the Kohan Gadol / the High Priest. Some Commands are just for the Priests. Some Commands are just for the Levites. Some Commands are for just farmers. Some Commands are just for children. The point is there are 613 Revelations of God's Light to us. Yet, no one is required to Observe all Taryag Mitzvot / 613 Commands. (Taryag equals 613 as noted.)

תריג
Taryag
ת 400
ר 200
י 10
ג 03

613

Each of us are accountable to Observe some of our Creator's Commands. It would be good for us to review all 613 Mitzvot of Ha Torah. Doing this would bring some Black and White to where we are. We would have a much better idea of what is expected of us. In addition to knowing the 613 Mitzvot, is the obedience each Mitzvot requires. This brings us to an extremely important question. How do any of us know when we sin? What tells us we have sinned?

The Christian Writings teach sin is a failure to do good. *To him that knows he should do good, and does not do good, it is sin*, James 4:17.

The Christian Scriptures teach all in humankind have failed. *'All have sinned, and come short of the glory of God,'* Romans 3:23.

Dear reader the Christian Scriptures define good as being subjective. So what I perceive as good, you may consider very very good. What you consider good, I may consider just barely fair. Christians allow for individuality and, emotion and instinctiveness to define sin. God does not leave sin up to our fluctuating emotions where by on one account you sinned and by another account you did not sin. The 613 Commands of the Torah teach what sin is. How can one repent from a sin that fluctuates. Sin is black and white. Repentance is black and white.

Again, I ask How do any of us know when we sin? What tells us we have sinned? How do we define sin? We define sin by Laws... We define sin by rules... Laws are important. We have been governed by laws from creation until now. Laws are good. In fact the Torah, i.e. the Law of the Lord is perfect. The Law restores us. This means repentance works within the structure of the Law. Being Jewish is a way of life. The Jewish way of life is governed by Ha Torah / The Torah. Jews are governed by 613 Laws of God. Yet, NOT ONLY JEWS are governed by Ha Torah. Everyone in this world is governed by the Torah to a degree!! Religions may debate their individual doctrines as much as they desire. That does not change the facts. The facts are that everyone one living is subject to Torah observance to a degree. I am saying that each of us live by the Grace of God but we are guided to a degree by Ha Torah. The legal systems of our world are guided by Ha Torah.

When a Jew runs a red light in their auto they have broken God's Law and the Government's Law. When a Christian runs a red light in their auto they have broken God's Law and the Government's Law. Dear Reader the Torah is a way of life. On the other hand, there are times when man's laws violate what God Commands. We see this more as society becomes liberal. The point is that not every law in society is based on Ha Torah. Yet, we can see Ha Torah's influence in government. The point is that when an individual observes Ha Torah they are normally in accord with society. Yet, there are differences.

Regardless, what we think or how we feel changes nothing. Our Creator Gave us rules to observe. Each of us will be accountable for obeying the Laws we are given. It has always been this way. It will always be this way. This may seem a little in one's face. It is not intended to.

Many who read this ALREADY FOLLOW many of the Commands of Ha Torah they are accountable for. For example: Most of us believe in God. We do not take God's Name in vain. We marry and have Children. We Teach them about God. We do not sleep with our mother, stepmother, aunt, daughter, daughter-in-law, sister etc. We do not sleep with our father, stepfather, uncle, brother, brother-in-law, son, step son etc. We try to not lie. We try not to steal. And the list of Mitzvot of

Commands from Ha Torah that we already observe goes on and on. So while it is true that we need to learn the 613 Commands of the Torah it is also true that we already observe many of Laws, REGARDLESS of our present religion. Even atheists who say they do not believe in God obey His Laws.

SUMMARY - We conclude with an affirmation that most of us abide by our Creators Commands. Yet, it was necessary to make the point we have Commands given to us by God that we need to follow. Those who are Jewish and those that may want to be Jewish are following the Creator's Commands to a degree.

Chapter Seven

Vision / Inspiration

The Seventh Concept Teaches our *present Torah portion* of the Bible was written by one very educated man with Vision Given by The Lord God..

In Israel none like Moses arose again. He is a prophet who clearly perceived His Vision.

Have you ever prayed to God for direction? Have you sought God? Have you cried out in tears to God begging for direction. Have you prayed, Oh Lord, please show me the way? Have you sought God for days, weeks, months or even years? Why did you seek God? It was because you desperately need something. It is good to cry out to God and to seek God. The difference between you and me and Moses is quite considerable. Most of us do not understand this. Human contact with the Creator is very limited. The Book of Genesis covers a time frame of 2,309 years. When we read the accounts of Genesis it is so easy to get the impression that humans had constant contact with God. This is an incorrect impression. Let me offer an example. From the time The Lord God Created Adam and Eve to the time of the flood which is 1,656 years The following had contact with God:

Adam's and Eve's recorded contact with God was about four times during 930 years. That is an average of about once every 232 ½ years. However these conversations took place all on the sixth day of Creation.
Genesis 1.28 – 30
Genesis 2.15 – 17
Genesis 2.20 – 22
Genesis 3.9 – 24

How about Noah? Noach had contact with God on about five different occasions over 950 years or about once every 190 years. See:
Genesis 6.13-21
Genesis 7.1-4

Genesis 7.16
Genesis 8.15
Genesis 9.1-17

Abraham had contact with God about eleven times... Check this out for yourself. Even when Moses was going back and forth to Pharaoh during the year 2447 F C God only spoke to him
Exodus 3.4 – 4.17
Exodus 5.22 – 6.9 Moses returned to the Lord
Exodus 6.10 – 6.13
Exodus 6.28 – 7.5
Exodus 7.8 – 7.9
Exodus 7.14 – 7.21
Exodus 7.26 – 7.29
Exodus 8.1 – 8.8 Moses Cried out to The Lord
Exodus 8.9 – The Lord Did as Moses Said
Exodus 8.12 -
Exodus 8.16 -
Exodus 8.26 – Moses Prayed to The Lord
Exodus 8.27 – The Lord Did as Moses Spoke
Exodus 9.1 – 9.5
Exodus 9.8 – 9.12
Exodus 9.13 – 9.21

Exodus 9.22 -
Exodus 9.33 Moses Spread His Hands out in Prayer to The Lord and the thunder ceased and the hail and rain did not reach the earth...
Exodus 10.1 – 10.2
Exodus 10.12
Exodus 10.18 Moses prayed unto The Lord
Exodus 10.19 The Lord Answered
Exodus 10.21
Exodus 11.1 – 11.8
Exodus 11.9
Exodus 12.1 – 12.27
Exodus 12.43 – 12.51

Exodus 12.51
And it came to pass the same day, that the Lord did bring the people of Israel out of the land of Egypt by their armies.

Dear Reader, during the twelve months Moses sought deliverance for the Children of Israel *the Torah Portion* of The Bible only records 29 communications between The Lord and Moses. The Lord initiated 24 of communications and

Moses just five. Notice that when Pharaoh would request Moses to pray for him after Moses left he would lift his hands towards the heavens and pray. Each time The Lord God responded. Dear One Moses was a Novie. Moses was a prophet. Moses' closeness with the Creator allowed him to say in advance what was going to happen. Moses would pray then the Creator backed the exact Prophetic Words of Moses.

Exodus 13.1- 13.2
And the Lord spoke to Moses, saying, Sanctify to me all the firstborn, whatever opens the womb among the people of Israel, both of man and of beast; it is mine.

The Creator speaks a few Words to Moses. Notice what Moses Says to the Children of Israel. Moses direction takes fourteen Verses. Why? This was another way our Creator Communicated with Moses. The Creator would Say several Words. Moses would receive an entire conversation from those few Words, immediately. No hesitation. Moses got the message immediately. Now dear reader the point to this discussion was to show God Spoke more to Moses than anyone in the Bible prior to this time or after this time. Yet, *the Torah portion* of the Bible records only 29 communications in one year.. In addition to this is the depth of each Word God Spoke to Moses was understood by Moses. This is why the Seventh Concept Teaches, **In Israel none like Moses arose again. He is a prophet who clearly perceived His Vision.**

Why?

Deuteronomy 34.7
And Moses was an hundred and twenty years old when he died: **his eye was not dim,** nor his natural force abated.

When *The Torah Portion* of the Bible Says Moses eye was not dim. The Torah is Saying the clarity of Moses Vision when he died was unchanged. His ability to prophecy clearly was unchanged. This CANNOT be said of any other writer of the

Bible.

Moses was raised as a prince of Egypt. He had the finest education. He was selected by God to serve when he was eighty years old. He served for forty years. This is what God Said about Moses:

Numbers 12. 5-8

And the Lord came down in the pillar of the cloud, and stood in the door of the Tabernacle, and called Aaron and Miriam: and they both came forth. And He Said, Hear now My Words: If there be a prophet among you, I the Lord Will Make Myself known unto him in a vision, and will speak with him in a dream. **[HOWEVER, with] My servant Moses this is not so, who is faithful in all mine house. With him will I Speak mouth to mouth,** *even apparently, and not in dark speeches; and the similitude of the Lord shall he behold: wherefore then were ye not afraid to speak against my servant Moses?*

Deuteronomy 34.10-12
And there *has not arisen since in Israel a prophet*

like Moses, whom the Lord knew face to face, In all the signs and the wonders, which the Lord sent him to do in the land of Egypt to Pharaoh, and to all his servants, and to all his land, And in all that mighty hand, and in all the great and awesome deeds which Moses performed in the sight of all Israel.

Dear Reader Moses only wrote the first Five Books of the Bible. These Five Books are *the Torah Portion* of the Bible. They have the HIGHEST INSPIRATION of any writer in the Bible as we will learn.

When I was young my father and mother, may they rest in peace, would drive from Denver to Mount Evens. From where we lived it is maybe a fifty mile drive. Mount Evens is part of the U.S. National Forest. The elevation of Mount Evans is 14,240 feet above sea level. Revi and I live about 550 feet above sea level.

When I was much younger almost sixty years ago the sky was crystal clear blue. Clouds were fluffy white. If your eyes were sharp you could see to downtown Denver, Colorado Springs, Pikes Peak. You could see hundreds of miles especially in the morning. Now a half century later haze and smog, etc., prevents the clear view I enjoyed as a child. It was amazing. It is very rare that visitors can see anything close to the clarity I saw as a child. Back in those days there was a gift shop / restaurant that has since burned down. Daddy would have a donut, a hot coffee black, Momma would have a donut, a hot coffee with cream and sugar, I would have a donut and hot chocolate, coco. Those days are forever gone as my father used to say, may they rest in peace.

I am trying to provide the reader with an understanding of the closeness and clarity Moses received from the Creator. Yet, there is nothing comparable to it. David, King of Israel, who likely had the next highest level of clarity wrote, as noted earlier, The Torah of The Lord is perfect.

Psalms 19.7 - 12

The Torah of the Lord is perfect, reviving the soul; the testimony of the Lord is sure, making wise the simple. The statutes of the Lord are right, rejoicing the heart; the commandment of the Lord is pure, enlightening the eyes. The fear of the Lord is clean, enduring for ever; the judgments of the Lord are true and righteous altogether. More to be desired are they than gold, even very fine gold; sweeter also than honey and the honeycomb. Moreover by them is your servant warned; and in keeping of them there is great reward.

In comparison to the Torah no other Book comes close. Only the Torah of The Lord is perfect.

SUMMARY – It is not common place to hear the Voice of The Lord. Even Moses during the twelve months while struggling, for the Children Of Israel's freedom in Egypt, ONLY received limited communication from the Lord. The Lord and Moses communicated 29 times. Yet, even though Moses was on the highest level of prophecy communication with the Lord was very limited.

Chapter Eight

Sefer Torah

In Judaism we realize the other Books in the Hebrew Scriptures have levels of Inspiration but none match the Torah. There is a VAST DIFFERENCE between a scroll from that of what scientist call manuscripts. The Torah was written on a scroll. The Torah Scroll was given great care and protection. Only a scribe can write a Torah Scroll. A properly cared for Sefer Torah Scroll will last between 300 to 400 years. This means today in 5773 we are only a little beyond eight Torah generations from when Moses received the Torah from our Creator.

In comparison The Christian Writings were written by anyone on pieces of paper that were widely circulated. I am not going to go into detail on this matter. It is up to you to read how poorly Christian Writings were handled. You may read about this in <u>Evidence that Demands A Verdict</u> or

Introduction to the Bible as noted earlier. The point is that both books state there are thousands of errors in the manuscripts of The Christian Writings. Why?

Years ago when I attended Bible College. The course Instructor taught us how carefully the Hebrew Scriptures were cared for and preserved. The custom of writing a Sefer Torah remains the same as thousands of years ago. The Sefer Torah is hand written. It is not printed by a printing press. It takes almost a year to write the Five Books by hand. The room had many writing tables, Kosher bird feather quills, ink, Kosher parchment, etc. There was a raised area where the Reader read The Torah from. The room was large.

The room next door was מִקְוֶה a Mikvah. A Mikvah is a bath used for ritual Immersion. Do you know what a Mikvah is? The Mikvah is a collection of water. A Mikvah may also be a lake, a river, a creek with constant running water. The water must never stop. A Mikvah within a city is constructed according to the Observances in the Torah. Generally speaking, The Mikvah is normally used ONLY by the Children of Israel. An exception is when when one converts to Judaism. Jewish women, married or single are supposed to do a ritual immersion immediately after bleeding, i.e. menstruation concludes, except on Sabbath or a Holiday. Observant Jews often use the Mikvah in the afternoon before Sabbath or a Holiday begins. A Sofer meaning Scribe סוֹפֵר would normally use the Mikvah each morning before morning prayers 24 / 7. Normally when an individual is unclean they must observe the ritual of immersion to become clean. Any of the following can cause uncleanness menstruation, childbirth, sexual relations, nocturnal emission, semen emission, emission of unusual bodily fluids, skin disease, death, and animal sacrifices. There is much more to the purpose and use of a Mikvah than this brief discussion.

A Sofer writes The Sefer Torah which is a hand written copy of the Five Books of Moses. A Sofer also writes Tefillin which are a set of tiny black leather boxes containing scrolls of parchment inscribed with verses from the Torah. Tefillin are worn every morning except on Sabbath and Holy Days. A Sofer writes the Mezuzot which are Scriptures written on Kosher Parchment and normally wrapped in a decorative box. A sofer also writes the ketubah which is a Jewish prenuptial agreement defining the rights and responsibilities of the groom, in relation to the bride. A sofer writes Megillot which are copies of the Book of Ruth, the Book of Lamentations, the Book of Ecclesiastes and the Book of Esther. A scribe has an extremely important responsibility. This is just a brief explanation to provide the Reader with a basic responsibility of a Sofer.

Now after making these brief explanations about the Mikvah and the Sofer lets return to the purpose of this discussion. Every table had a scribe. The reader would read a word. The scribes would write the Word in the exact same place. In the same column at the same height and in the same position. The reader would read another word. The same process was followed. When the reader approached the the Holy Name of The Lord the Scribes would stop exit the room go next door to the mikvah remove their clothing immerse themselves in the Mikvah then exit, dry and put on clean clothing. They would return to the room. The reader would say the Holy Name the scribes would write the Holy Name then stop. They would return to the Mikvah where they would repeat the process. What I was taught in Bible College omits some important details. In addition the Instructor did not give references on where he gathered this information. Yet the example provides an idea of what it is like to write a Sefer Torah.

Deuteronomy 31.19 Teaches us that every Jewish man has an obligation to write a Sefer Torah. Most of us are not on this level so we must employ a scribe to write a Sefer Torah for us or we might purchase a Letter or Word, etc. in a Sefer Torah that is being written. By many this obligation is considered to be the 613th Command of The Torah.

Being a scribe requires diligent study and the time to train and acquire the necessary skill to correctly write a Sefer Torah. One must learn the laws pertaining to composing a Torah Scroll. Being a righteous individual is at the forefront for anyone who would desire to write a Sefer Torah.

One learns the procedures required in advance to prepare the ink. One must learn about boiling oils, tar and wax and the precise mixture required with with tree sap, honey etc. One has to learn how to obtain kosher skins, how to prepare them, dry and store, etc. One has to score the skins to make lines and columns to follow.

One learns and practices Calligraphy. Assyrian script is used. One has to have a Kosher Sefer Torah to copy from. Do you have any idea of what this costs? Let's say a lot. About twenty years ago a Congregation purchased a used Sefer Torah for around $10,000.00. Then it cost another $600.00 for a computer scan for 100% accuracy. At about the same time a Scribe was employed to Write a Sefer Torah. That cost about $75,000.00. The point is that one either borrows a Sefer Torah or goes to a congregation and uses one on site.

A Scribe must go to the mikvah daily before morning prayers or before beginning his work. He must say a blessing when he begins and before he Writes the Holy Name of The Lord.

SUMMARY - The purpose of going into these details is to make the reader aware of the Holiness and the Separation a Scribe takes upon himself. I know a Scribe. We visited often when he lived in America. He practiced these customs. He went to a special school where he was taught how to be a scribe. He met with me and encouraged me to become a scribe.

Moses was greater than any of the scribes in the past or in the future. Can you imagine the greatness of Moses?

Dr. Geisler and Nix write in regards to the fidelity

of the Hebrew Scriptures. They list seven reasons. One of these reasons is the scrupulous rules of the Scribes. Another is the actual proof. In the Qumran caves copies of almost every Book of the Hebrew Scriptures were found. Some copies were dated as early as 3,200 years FC. This was only about seven hundred and fifty years from the Writing of the Sefer Torah by Moses. They were unchanged. The Chapters, the Words, the Letters were the same as today. Norman L. Geisler and William E. Nix, A General Introduction to the Bible (Chicago, Il. Moody Press, tenth printing 1977) p 358

Dear Reader I shared these meticulous details followed by Scribes in copying of The Torah portion of the Bible. This is why the Torah is Reliable. On the other hand the Christian Writings did not follow these practices and as a result suffer from many errors.

Chapter Nine

Comparing Writers

We are not going to review each Book of the Hebrew Scriptures or The Christian Writings individually but we will make some comparisons.

Joshua – Writer of the Book of Joshua. Who was he? He was Moses Minister. See Exodus 24.13 and Joshua 1.1.

Numbers 27.18 - 27
And the Lord said to Moses, Take Joshua the son of Nun, a man in whom is spirit, and lay your hand upon him; And set him before Eleazar the priest, and before all the congregation; and give him a charge in their sight. And you shall put some of your honor upon him, that all the congregation of the people of Israel may be obedient. And he shall stand before Eleazar the priest, who shall ask counsel for him according to the judgment of Urim before the Lord; at his word

shall they go out, and at his word they shall come in, both he, and all the people of Israel with him, all the congregation. And Moses did as the Lord commanded him; and he took Joshua, and set him before Eleazar the priest, and before all the congregation; And he laid his hands upon him, and gave him a charge, as the Lord commanded by the hand of Moses.

Deuteronomy 34.9
And Joshua the son of Nun was full of the spirit of wisdom; for Moses had laid his hands upon him; and the people of Israel listened to him, and did as the Lord commanded Moses.

Dear Reader we know who Joshua was. We read of his deep qualifications. He followed Moses for forty years then after proper training became the leader of the Children of Israel at the age of 92. Joshua lead Israel 28 years. Heninrich W. Guggenheimer, Seder Olam {A Jason Aronson Book, Lanham, Maryland; Rowman & Littlefield Publishers, Inc. 2005) pp 120-121

We know Solomon writer of Proverbs, Song of Solomon was King David's son. He is known for becoming the wisest man in the world. He requested of God, 'Give me wisdom and knowledge, that I may lead this people'... was the wisest man to live. See 2 Chronicles 1.7-11

Does the reader know that the Writer of The Book Ezra (Ezra), the Writer of the Book Nehemiah (Nehemiah), The Book of Esther, (Ezra and Mordechai), the Writer of the Book Daniel (Daniel), The Writer of The Book of Haggi (Haggi), The Writer of Zechariah (Zechariah), The Writer of Malachi (Malachi) each were members of the Great Assembly. They were among 120 members consisting of Prophets, Scribes and Sages. History of the Jewish People the Second Temple Era Mesorah Series, (Brooklyn New York: Mesorah Publications, Ltd. 9th Impression, 2003), p34

We could go on, David, King of Israel and Moses wrote much of the Psalms. How about Jeremiah, writer of Lamentations and Jeremiah, or Ezekiel writer of Ezekiel or Isaiah writer of Isaiah, we know these prophets.

Then we consider The Christian Writings of Matthew, Mark, Luke and John. Some Christian Scholars hold that the Book of Matthew was written by Matthew, who was one of the twelve apostles. I doubt it! However it is possible. Then there is the Book of Mark. Who wrote Mark? The writer of the Book of Mark is unknown? Christian Scholars suggest he may be John Mark but they don't know. Who is the writer of the Book of Luke? Christian Scholars don't know. According to Christian Scholars Dr. Luke may have been the traveling companion of Paul. The Book of John, i.e The Gospel of John was written by John the Apostle of Jesus, the son of Zebedee. He also wrote 1 John, 2 John, 3 John, and Revelations. 1Peter and 2 Peter were written by Peter the Apostle of Jesus. What do Christian writing say about Peter and John?

Acts 4:13

Now when they saw the boldness of Peter and John, and perceived that **they were unlearned and ignorant men,** *they marveled; and they took knowledge of them, that they had been with Jesus.*

Paul is accredited with writing Letters to Timothy, to Titus and to Philemon. They were like Spiritual sons to him. Paul wrote letters to The church in Rome (Romans), to the church at Corinth in Greece (1 and 2 Corinthians) and to the Galatians. Christian Scholars have several theories but cannot say for certain who Paul was addressing. Then there was the city of Ephesus (Ephesians), the city of Philippi (Philippians), The Town and Church in Colosse (Colossians)

The Books of Acts and Hebrews are unknown. The Book of James according to Christian Scholars who speculate, perhaps James is the brother of Jesus but we don't know. The Book of Jude is Jude. He describes himself as the brother of Jesus.

Paul claims to have sat at the feet of the great Rabbi Gamliel...

Acts 22.3
I am verily a man which am a Jew, born in Tarsus, a city in Cilicia, yet **brought up in this city at the feet of Gamaliel,** *and taught according to the perfect manner of the law of the fathers, and was zealous toward God, as ye all are this day.*

SUMMARY - Do we have anything that supports this? Does anyone confirm Paul's assertion? Do any of our Readers know who Rabbi Gamaliel is? Certainly Paul was better educated than others of the Christian Writings. Paul seems to be a bit self supporting. He tells the story of an alleged dream.

I knew a Messianic pastor. I believe he was a good man. He reminded me of Paul. He promoted himself. He had a following. I attended his Congregation for a while. One Sabbath I watched him as he went through this episode taken from the movie, 'The Chosen'. In the movie this Chasidic Rav acts like he has entered this superior spiritual trans. He freezes. His head is low. Then he begins to move into this dance. As I watched the Messianic Pastor do something like this I felt like he practiced these moves from this movie. Yet, I don't know... That week I did some investigation. I learned he was Pentecostal. He formed a group and appointed himself as the Bishop. Later he acquired a false conversion. He moved to Israel to do aliyah. He was there for awhile then deported.

To me it is very clear that the Christian Writings do not come close to the Spiritual Inspiration and Revelation as that of the Hebrew Scriptures. Then when I read of the 150,000 to 200,000 errors in the Christian Writings it is clear for me. God will never replace the Torah.

In Chapter Nine we compare a tiny amount of information of what we know about the Writers of the Hebrew Scriptures and the Writers of the Christian Testament. We do this because most individuals have not stopped to think about the

Writers and the influence they carry. If one is going to make outlandish claims that one book is done and the other Book is not they had better be able to answer serious questions in this chapter. We will examine which makes more sense. Superiority of one book is clear based upon the writers.

Chapter Ten

Truth

We are approaching a cross roads for those who would like to be Jewish. Do you know what a cross roads is? In this book it is Truth. For nine chapters I have shared true information about *the Torah Portion* of The Bible and religions of the world. At the end of this chapter it will be decision time.

Truth! What is the truth? For years I sought to find ways to fit all the pieces of the religious puzzle together. They don't fit! Think about it. There are individuals who love God and want to serve God. They are sincere. The Lord God wants to be loved, to be honored, to be served and most importantly to be obeyed. So why is there a problem? Where does the disagreement come from? In part, it is our perception of the Truth. Each religion wants followers to believe what they teach is the Truth.

Unfortunately we deceive our own selves. We read what the Bible says then we put a religious spin to the Verses we read. We re-interpret the Bible.

The disagreements we have come from how each of us evaluates. How do we reason? How do we disseminate an issue? How do we arrive at what we believe to be the Truth. What is the process and what are the steps of reasoning we use.

Believe is an unusual word. If one believes something then it has to be the Truth. We are absolutely convinced. We are confident! Nothing can persuade us. We believe it therefore it is true. One cannot realistically reason with a person who believes. A person who believes will not give an inch even though you show them the differences. They will not accept it!

In this book I have stated that I believe The Lord God has a plan for all humankind to follow. The plan is not based on the Bible. My belief is based on what I can see, what I can touch and what I can hear. My plan is not new. Abraham discovered God using this plan. Abraham came to believe in God based upon this plan.

Look at the world. Look at the sun, the moon the stars and planets. The earth spins in such away that we say the sun rises in the morning and sets in the evening. After awhile the moon and some stars appear. This happens everyday. This is normal to us.

The movement of the sun, the moon and the stars are consistent to the second. We know exactly when the sun will rise and set. We know when the moon will be full. We know when there will be an eclipse. We know this information in advance because there is an order that the sun, moon and stars function within. God established the order that our day, week, month and year come and go. We don't think twice about it. The universal plan works everyday just as God designed it to.

Dear reader by the age of ten each of us have experienced 3,650 plus sun rises and sun sets. We observe there is a design. We observe there is a plan. We can see the plan. We can make plans by the plan.

Now this being the situation lets take the human body. By the age of ten we have seen the human body function for 3,650 days. We should know something about the human body. We can see the human body was uniquely designed.

I am waiting for those who believe in evolution to explain DNA...

When we think of truth do we have the space to allow for possibilities outside of our own belief? With limited knowledge we can see that God designed a plan for the earth to follow. God designed a plan for our bodies to follow. It is therefore reasonable to expect God to have a plan from the beginning for humankind to follow. Knowing this we should be able to understand that an organized God would not Create Adam and Eve without a plan. What sense does it make for God to have an organized plan that the universe follows but when it comes to humankind there is no plan. God designed our bodies and our souls. Why would He not have a plan for us? The fact is that God does have a plan for humankind to follow.

SUMMARY - Dear Reader just because we may not know about God's plan does NOT mean it did not exist. If other religions do not speak of God's Plan From The Beginning that does not mean there was no plan. The Truth is God Has always had a plan. In these first ten chapters we have shown many possibilities from different angles. Each shows that God had a plan. We have provided a number of references that establish a plan existed. We have also proven the absolute absurdity of the teachings from other religions which say the Hebrew Scriptures are fulfilled, done away with and are not longer valid for our time.

While we are on the subject let me point out that

before the beginning God's plan provided repentance, for every human being, forgiveness for any and ALL our errors and eternal life for each of us. From the day our souls were spoken into life, i.e. assigned names on the second day of creation every name was entered into the Book of Life. Do you have any idea of how difficult it is to have your name erased from the book of Life?

And again we inquire what does God want? God wrote our names in the Book of Life. We do not have to earn this. Our names are already written in the Book of Life. What we should be concerned with is the word *erased*... We do not want our name erased.

In the second Book of this series, God Willing we will discuss God's Plan of Salvation, How God handles our mistakes, i.e. How we receive forgiveness for our sins, what happens at death and life after death. These subjects have been grossly misrepresented by some religions. As we will learn God's Plan is easy to learn and to follow. Join me in the second book of <u>Would You Like To Be Jewish</u>?

I invite you to join class discussions on this subject at bnti.us. Look for Would you like to be Jewish? Click on the link.

ABOUT THE AUTHOR

Dr. Akiva Gamliel Belk

Jewish, Husband, Father, Grandfather and Step Great Grandfather.

Graduate:
A.A. Long Beach City College,
B.A. Southern California Bible College,
M.A. Southern California Theological Seminary,
D. Th. Southern California Theological Seminary,
D. Th. Denver Charismatic Theological Seminary

Individual Study:
Rabbi Dovid Nusbaum,

Bais Medrash at Yeshiva Toras Chaim,
Hornosteipler Rebbe, Mordicai Tewerski
Group Study:
Rabbi Yaakov Meyer, Aish Denver
Rabbi Yisroel Engel, Director, Colorado Chabad.

Founder:
Jewishpath.org
Jewishlink.net
7commands.com
Buntings

Dean of Jewish Studies
B'nai Noach Torah Institute, LLC – Biblical Online Studies

Author of various books.
bnti.us/books.html

Businessman:
Realtor and Property Investor

www.ingramcontent.com/pod-product-compliance
Lightning Source LLC
LaVergne TN
LVHW051837080426
835512LV00018B/2922